CHANPURU

CHANPURU

Reflections and Lessons from the Dojo

Garry Parker

TAMBULI MEDIA

www.TambuliMedia.com
Spring House, PA USA

DISCLAIMER

The author and publisher of this book are NOT RESPONSIBLE in any manner whatsoever for any injury that may result from practicing the techniques and/or following the instructions given within. Since the physical activities described herein may be too strenuous in nature for some readers to engage in safely, it is essential that a physician be consulted prior to training.

First Published April 01, 2015 by Tambuli Media
Copyright @ 2015 by Garry Parker

ISBN-13: 978-1-943155-05-7
ISBN-10: 1943155054
Library of Congress Control Number: 2015935607

All Rights Reserved. No part of this publication may be reproduced or utilized in any form or by any means, electronic or mechanical, including photocopying, recording, or by any information storage and retrieval system, without prior written permission from the Publisher or Author.

Edited by Jody Amato
Cover and Interior by Summer Bonne

Acknowledgments

With deepest gratitude to my teacher and mentors for guiding me on this path, and for encouraging me not to fill their very footsteps, but to follow them on the same path on which they traveled, leaving my own imprint.

Takamiyagi Hiroshi Sensei with his relentless thirst for knowledge, tireless research into the roots of karate, and the genuine compassionate heart of a warrior, certainly embodies the old maxim: *Do not seek to follow in the master's footsteps; seek what they sought.*

Thank you to my wife Izumi for tolerating my late nights, and for providing an endless supply of coffee with a smile on her face. Thank you to my mentors and friends who encouraged me, my family that supported me, and to those that I've encountered along my martial arts journey.

Finally, I would like to thank my publisher Tambuli Media, and Dr. Mark Wiley, for guiding me throughout this process every step of the way; his faith in this project, his patience in editing and meeting my needs, and his ability to gently nudge me in the right direction have contributed to the completed book that you have in front of you.

Each one of you, in different ways, are responsible for my continuous drive, ambition and zeal.

Praise for *Chanpuru*

"The honesty that pervades from this book comes from Parker's total immersion in the Okinawan culture. His metamorphosis from American GI to Okinawan Karate Man gives readers a unique understanding of martial arts from the Ryukyu Kingdom."

—Gary Gabelhouse
Novelist and Goju-ryu karate practitioner

"Fascinating and important lessons from a man who lived and trained in a place most people only every dream about. I highly recommend this book to all who study traditional Okinawan and Japanese martial arts."

—Joe Swift
Tokyo Mushinkan Dojo - Japan

"There are lots of reasons to choose this read, but one in particular makes this book a rare find among the masses. Garry Parker's sensei, Takamiyagi Hiroshi, is a true master of Okinawan Karate, one who has spent much of his life of Karate study, and also learning a Chinese system from the source... this book gives the reader access to this experience, a way to learn from Garry Parker's personal journey. As a glimpse into the cultures, training, methods, and daily life from the perspective of "an American student in Okinawa," it's a great opportunity to see how all the parts actually connect."

—Wade Chroninger
Meibukan Okinawa Dojo - Okinawa

Garry Parker gives the rest of us a glimpse into the process he went through, as a young American serviceman, learning not only the language and the customs of a foreign country, but also fully engaging in the process of actually *understanding* the culture that birthed one of the most popular forms of martial art on the planet. I believe that reading *Chanpuru* will help solidify all karateka's basics, as (in my opinion) the foundation of karate is formed on the relationships one develops in the dojo.

—Russ Smith
Burinkan Dojo - Florida USA

Table of Contents

Foreword by Hiroshi Takamiyagi xi

Foreword by Dr. Mark Wiley xiii

Author's Preface xv

BOOK ONE REFLECTIONS 1

    Chapter 1: Okinawa 3
        Haisai 3
        Hamagawa Dojo 7
        Makiwara Sensei 14
        Survival 15
        Civilian Life 17
        Matsuri 19
        Ichariba Chodee 22
        Ganbatte! 23
        The Sunabe Seawall 24
        Not Your Black Belt 26
        Kantoku 28
        Every Day Is a Test 30
        Chuura Umi 31
        Okinawa Time 32

    Chapter 2: Home Again 35
        Culture Shock 35
        A New Chapter 36
        Breaking New Ground 39
        Keys to the Kingdom 40

    Chapter 3 43
        Kazoku Dojo 43

BOOK TWO LESSONS 51

    Chapter 4: Training 53
        Train Anyway 53

Do vs. Jutsu 55
Challenge Your Comfort Zone 58
Your Own Path 59
Playing Karate 60
Training with Injuries 61
Forging the Blade 62
A Full Cup of Tea 63

Chapter 5: Rambling 65
Ronin 65
The Bridge 66
Thoughts on Tradition (Part 1) 68
Thoughts on Tradition (Part 2) 70
Old School 72

Chapter 6: Students 75
Coming Home 75
Giri — The True Student/Teacher Connection 77
Giri Explained 78
An Open Letter to Students 79
Talk is Cheap 81
Next Time 81
The Timeless Dojo 83

Chapter 7: Teachers 85
Sensei's Hat 85
Gratitude 86

Chapter 8: Character 89
Prejudice in the Dojo 89
Out of Order 91
Moments that Define You 92

Chapter 9: Shin (The Mind) 95
Beginner's Mind 96
Remaining Mind 96
Empty Mind 97
Kaizen 97

Chapter 10: Growth 99
    Baggage 99
    Fifteen 100
    Letting Go 103
    Be the Best 104
    After the Rain 105
    Matsu 107

Chapter 11: Life 109
    A Beautiful Thing 109
    Fishing 110
    Last Sunrise 111
    Passing the Torch 113

BOOK THREE LEGACY 115

Chapter 12: Legacy 117
    Making History Abroad 123
    Junbi (Preparation) 124
    USA Arrival 126
    First Class 129
    Appointment 132
    Gasshuku 139
    One Chance 146
    First Interview 147
    Going Home 150

Epilogue 153

Glossary 155

About the Author 163

Foreword

Garry Parker lived in Okinawa from 1990 to 1996 and trained diligently at my Okinawa Goshukan Dojo. Even after returning to the United States, he has been devoted to training and sharing Shuri-te and Gosoken (Five Ancestor Kenpo) at every opportunity.

The Okinawa Goshukan Columbus Dojo is filled with the excitement of its many students. They are surrounded by people who train in other budo (martial arts), including Nihon Judo and Mugairyu Iaido, and who enjoy sharing their experiences and training with each other.

This is especially true for Judo. Mr. Parker began training with Schmitt sensei since 1984. He trained many years longer in Judo than in Karate, and although he primarily practices Karate-Do now, his years of Judo experience has assisted his development of tactical Karate in the areas of *tuidi*, and his foundation in the Judo style shines through.

The visions of the Columbus Dojo training camps (Gasshuku) shows many people who are very serious in training in Okinawan and Japanese martial arts. When I see their passionate, sincere, and faithful training, it reinforces my own passion. You can tell that the atmosphere of the American dojo is full of dreams of becoming proficient in Okinawan and Japanese budo by the practitioners respectful attention.

Mr. Parker has been gallantly searching for the path through his training and this has led to his success, and he has now published his book looking back at the experiences of his extensive Bushido training.

One might say that "ten years can bring a lot of changes." It seems like time has flown by like an arrow, and I was happy to be present as Parker's Columbus Dojo celebrated its 15th Anniversary. I believe Mr. Parker has had many valuable training experiences in the field of martial arts. As a person who taught him Shuri-te and Gosoken (Five Ancestor Kenpo), I feel deeply about him publishing this book and I would like to send my heartfelt praise for him. I am looking forward to seeing the published version.

The Parker family is a very happy and successful family. More than anything, they are very fortunate to have a whole family that is dedicated to karate; this is a rare occurrence. Mrs. Izumi Parker supports her husband in every aspect, and their children, Lisa, Kaori and Kenji are all following in their father footsteps with their devotion to karate. I would like them to continue these exceptional ways of life.

Mr. Parker and my son (Naoki) are about the same age and they trained hard side-by-side together as young men in Okinawa. He now is in his mid-forties and in his prime, and I feel he is like my son. As his sensei, I would like to encourage him by sending these words *"Ai wa ai yori irete ai yori aoshi,"* which means, "Some pupils surpass their masters."

In Okinawa dialect, we say *"Uya masain guwa."* What a parent wishes should be the same no matter where it is.

Additionally, one should not be satisfied with their commitment to karate practicing in their forties and fifties. It is very important to firmly maintain karate-do well into one's sixties and seventies, hopefully even into one's eighties and nineties. This is Ryukyu's traditional way of life and way of being as a *bujin*, or a true warrior. It is common knowledge that leaders of Shuri-te live long lives. In the time when the average man lived fifty years, many bujin lived to be eighty to ninety years old.

Its technique is a low-impact way where "small can beat big." This is why Shuri-te has been perfected to its best over its long history. Understandably, the skillful bushi embraces this ideal way. Traditionally, expert skill accounts for much more than being strong and firm.

Because we are master and pupil, I did not want my words to simply sound like an official greeting or statement; I wanted to convey my true feelings. Congratulations on publishing your book. I hope this is a great turning point for you and I wish you to continue to be a source of great inspiration in the near future.

—Takamiyagi Hiroshi
Okinawa Goshukan-Ryu Karate-Do< Senior Advisor
Chatan-Cho, Okinawa-Japan
September 24, 2014

Foreword

Since childhood, I've been fascinated with traditional martial arts and the many journeys one can take along their paths.

Among my favorite books are those where the author shares his experience in finding a teacher, in becoming accepted as a student, and in training the traditional way. Others are those containing insights into the cultural and spiritual aspect of the arts. Garry Parker's *Chanpuru* offers all of this.

I feel a kinship with Garry Parker. He met his sensei, Takamiyagi Hiroshi, and I met my sifu, Alexander Co, around the same time. What's more, Takamiyagi traveled from Okinawa to the Philippines to meet Co, since they share practice in Fukien Five Ancestor Fist. Garry has become Takamiyagi's disciple, responsible for upholding his art in the United States; and I have become the same for Co. And so, what a pleasure it is to publish Garry's book.

In *Chanpuru*, Parker takes us along on his Okinawan karate journey. "When I arrived at the Naha Airport for the very first time," he begins... and then the reader is hooked, wants to know what happens next. Being accepted into a foreign physical cultural like traditional karate is rare for Westerners. As Parker's account attests, the traditional dojo is very unlike the modern "karate school" with mats and air-conditioning and birthday parties. It is about self-development, self-knowledge, and respect. Like Itosu Anko Sensei wrote, *"Karate begins and ends with respect."* Not trophies, no colored belts.

Parker shows us there are "no excuses on the path of karate." Training hard and being respectful are the ways forward. Traditional Okinawan karate is a bridge to the past. Unfortunately, the bridge is crumbling and the past is fading. Garry Parker took the time to earn his way into a traditional karate culture, and now holds the torch for others to see the way. *Chanpuru*'s lessons and insights are timeless as the Okinawan culture.

—Mark V. Wiley
Publisher, Tambuli Media
March 25, 2015

Author's Preface

From the beginning of time, mankind has had to invent and progressively adapt methods of protection to survive. To ensure the survival of our species against wild animals, and to ensure survival of family bloodlines against ruthless thieves and marauders, we as humans have had to fight to survive. Centuries ago, we discovered that the most efficient way to protect ourselves was to create distance from the enemy; when the distance was closed and contact was unavoidable, the great equalizer was often weapons. From the rudimentary club to the masterfully crafted razor sharp sword, we improvised, created, and evolved through trial and error with bloodshed and sacrifice, into the warriors of today.

Fast forward to the Ryukyu Kingdom of the 1600s. The indigenous martial arts of Okinawa (known originally as *ti*) were blended with the fighting arts of Fujian China to formulate the birth of what would become the globally popular martial art known as Okinawan Karate.

Before uniforms, belts, titles, and the tradition of a dojo with wooden floors, were quiet warriors in everyday clothes, secretly training in backyards or behind walls, diligently practicing under the cloak of night. There were no tournaments, no politics, and no nonsense; there were only hard men that sacrificed time, sleep, and comfort to toughen their bodies and strengthen their spirit in pursuit of improving their odds at protecting themselves and their loved ones in the absence of weapons. A nation of disarmed citizens, no matter how peaceful, will always find a way to improvise and protect themselves. The Okinawan karate legends of centuries past set the bar high, and we still follow in their footsteps.

The key turning point for Okinawan Karate's popularity in America came courtesy of the American military men following World War II. During the American occupation of Okinawa after the war, Soldiers, Marines, and Airmen began to practice karate. For the economically struggling karate teachers, this was an answer to prayer; teaching American servicemen meant food and clothing for the Okinawan teachers' families. After training a few years, many of the servicemen went back to the United States, continued, training, and opened dojo of their own. These men were the pioneers of karate in America. Those were the glory days of Karate in the West! The 1950's through the 1970s saw an enormous explosion in popularity of karate in the United States. Brutally hard contact, gallons of sweat pooled on the floor from hours of practice, blood and tears shed, bumps, bruises, and the occasional broken nose, black eye, bloody lip, or fractured toe was just an ordinary part of training. You would get bruised and banged up; this type of training was expected, and it was unapologetically accepted as the only way to train. Without the constant testing of skills within the four wall of the dojo, a karateka could not be confident that he was learning an effective art.

What happened?

Slowly, things began to change. Now, we see a softer, gentler, approach to Okinawan karate. We see lighter contact, shorter training sessions, and lightning fast promotions. In fact, if not for the sign on the door, or the photos on the wall, many Okinawan karate dojo in America could easily be mistaken for their Korean counterparts. There is no denying that the new generation of Karate is here to stay; we live in a society of instant gratification. With the advent of technology in the late 20th Century, popular culture has helped groom an entire generation of impatient people that want it now, and are willing to pay extra to get it. There are 'karate schools' that advance or promote students with very little skill improvement. Rewards for mediocrity and promotions for simply showing up have become all too common.

Fortunately, that isn't the case with all dojos; the old style of Okinawan karate training actually seems to be enjoying a revival since the beginning of the 21st Century. There are still those that hold on to the old traditions and practice them diligently. There are those who train quietly, dedicated to preserving the old karate of Okinawa, and they can't be swayed or bought with the promise of money, titles, or fame.

I consider myself fortunate to have met and trained with such men and women, and have dedicated my life to the practice and pursuit of the karate of times past. To the traditional karate that can only be found in small dojos in unassuming places, sometimes off the beaten path, and often only with an invitation or personal introduction from a current student or respected teacher. In the chapters that follow, I invite you to come along on my journey and see how this American gained entrance to a rapidly disappearing society of authentic Okinawan martial arts seldom seen in today's world; a journey that has brought me a lifetime of rewards that money can't buy.

I'll guide you on my journey, both in and out of the dojo, and introduce you to the experience through my eyes; the journey can be a little personal, and isn't always about karate, but that is what makes a memorable life. All experiences on my path haven't been glorious, but they all have helped to forge my will.

This book is divided into 3 sections: Book One is autobiographical, in that this section details highlights and reflections of my personal journey in karate from the dojo floor to the crashing waves of the East China Sea, and all points between.

Book Two is filled with topics relevant to the study and practice of this art. This includes lessons that I've learned, essays, advice, personal thoughts and stories, and little nuggets of wisdom that I've been taught along the way, and am now passing on to you.

Book Three is dedicated to the legacy of my teacher, Takamiyagi Hiroshi, the founder of Goshukan-Ryu (the martial arts style comprised of Goso Kenpo, or Five Ancestor Fist, and Shuri-Te), and pioneer of Wu Zu Quan (aka Ngo Cho Kun or Chinese Five Ancestor Boxing) on Okinawa, Japan. An exclusive interview is included in this chapter, along with rare photos from his personal collection.

This book is written for everyone, and no one in particular, in that the target audience for this work is very broad; it is my sincere desire that karateka of all ages and skill levels will be able to identify with some of the content, or perhaps even learn something new. Unlike the early years veiled in secrecy, now Okinawan Karate is for everyone, and should be freely shared with all.

So what is the meaning of *chanpuru*, the title of this book? It is one of the most popular dishes in Okinawa; there is no set style, or list of ingredients for this amazingly simple, yet wildly popular dish. It usually consists of some type of meat, lots of fresh vegetables, tofu, and egg. This is all thrown together and sautéed (stir-fried) and served with rice.

Chanpuru simply means something thrown together, or mixed up, and while there is usually a common elemental flavor, there is also a vast variety of combinations that can be enjoyed.

Indeed, chanpuru is the embodiment of the Ryukyu and Okinawan experience; with the cultures of China, Siam, Taiwan, and Japan blended into one; the flavor is uniquely Okinawan, while highlighting the very best flavors of each contributing culture.

This book is similar to Okinawa chanpuru. The common theme is Karate, but there are many different elements pertaining to the subject. These elements are compiled in this small book as a series of tips, philosophy, articles, advice, and experiences that I have gained over a lifetime of practicing martial arts. From a high school student practicing judo at the Columbus, Georgia YMCA, to a young American living in Okinawa, my experiences have taught me to be a better student, and hopefully, a better teacher.

It is my sincere wish that every person reading this book will gain something positive; In a time where stylistic elitism is still rampant within the traditional martial arts community, this book is directed toward everyone, and no-one in particular. The content of this book is written for all karateka — for those that don't train, or those inactive practitioners on a lengthy break, perhaps a chapter or two will even help inspire you to go to the dojo and take steps on the path to mastering your own destiny.

—Garry Parker
Columbus, Georgia
July 2014

BOOK ONE

REFLECTIONS

CHAPTER 1

Okinawa

Haisai

When I arrived at the Naha Airport the very first time, I had no idea what to expect; it was winter, and having just left Korea, I was prepared for the worst possible weather; obviously I hadn't properly researched Okinawa when I received my PCS (permanent change of station) orders to "Kadena Air Base, Japan."

As I stepped into the airport, I was met with a huge sign that read "Haisai Okinawa" in bright colors with two animated, smiling Shisa (lion-dogs) on either side. As I gathered my baggage, I noticed flowers everywhere; huge red and yellow hibiscus, along with the native *deigo* (akabana) flower adorned the

Higa-San, Parker, Takamiyagi Sensei in Shuri Village 2003

> When a foreigner dedicates a little time and effort to learn about their native culture, the beautiful spirit of the Okinawan people is revealed.

Naha Airport in vivid color. What a pleasant surprise! I was just another young airman reporting to my new duty station; little did I know that this would be the first step of the journey that would change my life forever.

Haisai is the Uchinaguchi (Okinawan language) word for 'hello'. This greeting is used everywhere, and in addition to being a fairly simple word to learn, I found it to be a great ice-breaker when meeting new people, or even when visiting a shop, business, or restaurant. I discovered that Haisai, to the Uchinanchu, is not just a greeting, but an integral part of their culture. Haisai is a connection to their family, their grandparents, their past, and their roots. Haisai helps the Uchinanchu to preserve their unique identity as distinctly different from the Japanese that occupied their tiny island Ryukyu Kingdom and attempted to strip them of their unique culture as they imposed imperial rule.

Parker and Takamiyagi Sensei. Shuri-Okinawa 2003

Parker and Takamiyagi Hiroshi, Shuri Gusuku 2003

As an American living in Okinawa - the simple act of bowing, smiling, and saying 'Haisai' opened dialogue for me that otherwise may never have happened. The *Uchinanchu* are friendly, but they are also extremely proud of their heritage. When a foreigner dedicates a little time and effort to learn about their native culture, the beautiful spirit of the Okinawan people is revealed. I can't begin to count the number of times that a dismissive or suspicious look was transformed instantly to a smile because I spoke one little word. I was invited into the homes and lives of some wonderful people that I certainly would never have met, all because of Haisai.

Now, before you get the idea that Haisai is a magical word that transforms Uchinanchu into friendly, sharing people that naively invite foreign strangers into their homes, it isn't. Let me explain: It is the principle of the word, not the actual word that opens doors. Anyone who is sincere and makes the effort to learn the language and culture of Okinawa, is usually readily accepted by the

Uchinanchu. After a few years, I realized that, in some places, I was even more accepted than the *naichaa* (mainland Japanese)!

> For me, the black belt was an unattainable goal, yet I did it, and I was the first American to do so in the Hamagawa Dojo.

One particular Sunday morning, I loaded up my Toyota Hi-Ace van with snorkeling gear to start another new adventure; I discovered so much of the island by driving around and attempting to get lost. Away from Highway 58 and the main roads, driving up north through the small villages, stopping here and there, I discovered the real Okinawa. This particular morning, I was planning to go snorkeling in Onna-son (just past Yomitan) and decided to go to Ie-Jima; I drove all the way there and just got to the bridge when the rain started; After a half hour or so, the rain turned to a heavy storm, and my snorkeling adventure was cancelled. I started back toward Kadena.

Along the way I stopped at a roadside stand near *Manzamo* (a popular tourist attraction) for lunch; I noticed that not only was I the only gaijin (foreigner), but all the other customers seemed to be naichaa! The staff greeted me with a canned 'irrashaimase' (Welcome) and I nodded a bow. I returned the greeting with *"Hasai, Chabidasai"* (hello, forgive the intrusion). The Obasan's (old woman's) eyes lit up, a huge ear-to-ear grin appeared, and she replied with a loud *"Haisai! Mensore!"* (Hello! Welcome!) I replied with '*Nifedebiru!*' (Thank you!) She then called me over to the side, out of line, and sat me at the counter and served the biggest bowl of *soki-soba* (a distinctly Okinawan pork spare-rib-flavored noddle soup) I had ever seen. The day was stormy and gloomy, but I found a little piece of sunshine that day with the older woman at the roadside stand for lunch; we talked sporadically for a couple of hours, whenever she had a few minutes between her other customers. I had exhausted nearly all of the Uchinaguchi in my linguistic arsenal within the first couple of minutes, but had a working knowledge of Nihongo (the Japanese language). She was extremely interested in why I, a young American serviceman, was taking such an interest in her culture. The first couple years of learning and studying the language and culture were sometimes a struggle, but that day on the side of the road, I no longer felt like an outsider, I felt at home.

Hamagawa Dojo

The Hamagawa Dojo was a small, unassuming building covered with vegetation and tucked away on a tiny corner lot in a residential neighborhood only a few hundred meters from the Sunabe sseawall. Compared to the houses and apartment buildings, the dojo seemed out of place. Little did I know when I stepped in for the very first time, that this little hot metal building would forever change my life! My friend Wade had been married several months before, and it was at his wedding that I was introduced to Takamiyagi Sensei. Wade and I talked, and trained a little, he was a student at the Hamagawa

Original Hamagawa Dojo Kanban: 1990

Hamagawa Dojo Entrance: 1990

Side of the Hamagawa Dojo: 1990

Dojo, and lived in the apartments across the street, but had previously trained in kenpo (Okinawan karate) back home in New Mexico. After meeting Takamiyagi Sensei and watching the karate demonstration at Wade's wedding I expressed interest, and he introduced me to the sensei.

At one point, there were four of us from the same squadron training at the Hamagawa Dojo; Wade, Mark, Dave, and me. Within a month or two, Mark and Dave lost interest, and Wade eventually left to practice at another dojo; then I was the only American left in the Dojo.

For a few months after that, the reception from my *senpai* (senior classmate) was a little colder, and I felt that Takamiyagi Sensei wasn't sure if I was really committed; over the years, American servicemen had gained a reputation in Okinawa for dojo-hopping, or moving from one dojo to another every few months without fully committing to one.

I made a commitment to arrive early and stay late at the dojo; I trained every day, after work and on weekends; I practiced *kihon* (basics) for hours, I stretched, and practiced the one kata that I was learning. After a couple of

Takamiyagi Sensei leading Kata practice at the Hamagawa Dojo. The author is back row, closest to the camera.

months, the reception began to grow warmer from my senpai and Takamiyagi Sensei gave me more personalized attention and correction. I learned in a few months what some Americans never learn; until you prove your dedication and loyalty, you won't receive any detailed instruction or interaction. I learned

that I had to work hard to be accepted as a true student at the Hamagawa Dojo. I had to earn it.

Throughout the years, I absorbed some of the essence of that dojo, and did my part to add to the spirit of the dojo, too. Countless gallons of sweat poured down my body and soaked into the hardwood floor as I practiced and learned all that I could absorb.

> Throughout the years, I absorbed some of the essence of the dojo, and did my part to add to the spirit of the dojo, too.

Blood from my shins was wiped from the tire *makiwara* (striking post) as I practiced perfecting my *mawashi-geri* (round kick). Blood from my knuckles soaked into the leather *sunabukuro* (striking sandbags) and makiwara cover, as I trained impatiently, trying to do too much, too fast, and injuring myself in the process. Tears of frustration were shed when I struggled to perfect *waza* (strikes) or *kata* (forms), but just couldn't get it, in spite of my efforts. Years later, tears of joy were hidden by my sweat-drenched face as I received my shodan (black belt). I never thought I would get that far.

Everything I've accomplished in martial arts is due to hard work and diligent practice. I was never very athletic, and always had to work harder than most to achieve the same result. For me, the black belt was an unattainable goal; yet I did it, and I was the first American to do so in the Hamagawa Dojo. Before then, I was already a dedicated student; but after my *shodan* promotion, my loyalty to my teacher and my dojo was solidified. I made a

Hamagawa Dojo 1995: L-R Isa, Takamiyagi Naoki, Author, Takamiyagi Hiroshi.

Hamagawa Dojo 1995: Nafudakake (name-boards of current students)

commitment then to remain a loyal and dedicated student as long as I was living and breathing.

For the next 18 months following my black belt promotion, I continued to train, learn, and absorb all that I could process in such a short period of time. I took every opportunity to practice, learn and receive all knowledge that Takamiyagi Sensei would share with me. Sure, I was just one of thousands of foreigners training in karate that had come to Okinawa courtesy of the United States government, but seeing my name within the *Yudansha* (black belt) ranks on the *Nafudakake*, the only name in katakana, made me realize how far I had come.

> makiwara... this simple tool forges the spirit of determination, ensures proper patience, and breaks bad habits without prejudice.

Attending testing days now took on a different meaning for me. After my shodan promotion, I was no longer nervous on testing days, for it was the first time in years that I was able to observe and fulfill my duty as senpai by helping my *kohai* (juniors).

Takamiyagi Sensei offering critique after testing. 1995

Students enjoying refreshments after testing. 1995

Makiwara Sensei

The most intimidating attack on my senses as a brand new karate student was the *makiwara* (striking post); I watched as my senpai hit that board over and over again. Each strike brought a loud "thump" or "thwack" depending on which one was being used; One was more flexible and had a "thwack" sound when struck; the other was much firmer and resonated with a deep loud "thump." We were encouraged to train on the makiwara every time we were in the dojo; I didn't ask questions, I simply gave the standard "Hai Sensei" and followed orders. Corrections were given and details of body mechanics, alignment, and power generation were taught. Little by little, I learned from my mistakes, and gained enough skill and confidence to make my own "makiwara music."

Being young and inexperienced, I made the same mistakes that many impatient young men have made, and paid the price with bloody knuckles, injuries, and standing in front of my NCOIC (non-commissioned officer in charge) more than once, to explain my scabbed and swollen knuckles. Like many young servicemen at that time, I presumed that large protruding knuckles were expected as side effect of hard and heavy makiwara training; I pushed way past my limits, didn't allow enough time to heal after injury. The results were disproportionately large and protruding knuckles, and I was

proud of them too! Now I looked like a real karate man… or so I thought. One evening after class, I stopped in the store around the corner from the dojo for a refreshing Aquarius Neo, my favorite sports drink at the time. As I was waiting in line to pay for my drink, an older lady behind me began to strike up a conversation. She asked me where I practiced (I was sweaty and still wearing my gi (uniform) pants and a t-shirt), and I told her that I trained at the Hamagawa Dojo around the corner. She grabbed me by the hand and ran her thumb across my knuckles:

"You're still a beginner, aren't you?" How did she know that?

"Hai, roku ka getsu mai kara hajimarimashita (I only started about six months ago*)."*

"Jaa, mada wakaran, ne. Mouto yuukuri dayo; Amari isogan-de (Well, you don't understand yet. Don't be in such a rush)."

"Hai, nifuedebiru." It was my turn at the register, so I paid and left. To this day, I don't know who the old lady was, but she certainly knew more about karate than I did. Perhaps her husband or father was a teacher, who knows. Her advice stuck with me, and bothered me so much that I arrived extra early at the next class to speak to Takamiyagi Sensei about it. I told him what had transpired, and asked if it was true. Sensei just laughed and shook his head. "I told you already, but you listen to an old lady." Wait, I don't remember Sensei, *gomen-nasai* (I'm sorry). Takamiyagi Sensei then reminded me that he had told me on day one to be patient, avoid injury, and build up gradually. I vaguely remembered that conversation, apologized again, then excused myself to go train.

> There are many teachers that we'll encounter throughout our martial arts journey, but none as strict and unforgiving as the makiwara.

There are many teachers that we'll encounter throughout our martial arts journey, but none as strict and unforgiving as the makiwara. You can't cheat on the makiwara. You can't force results. I have found that the mistakes I've made in distance, timing, or alignment were immediately corrected by the makiwara. This simple tool forges the spirit of determination, ensures proper patience, and breaks bad habits without prejudice.

Survival

When my contract for World Airways expired, I found myself without sponsorship, and only 30 days left on my work visa to transition or to leave Okinawa. After so much sacrifice and so much progress on my personal karate journey, my world was crumbling in front of my eyes. I wasn't sure which direction to go, but I knew I wasn't ready to go back home to the USA. On the advice of an acquaintance, I booked a round-trip flight to Guam in order to receive a 90 day visitor stamp on my passport. This bought me enough time

> Although I immersed myself daily with all things Okinawan, this was a lonely time in my life with no other daily American interaction.

to secure employment and apply for another visa once I returned to Okinawa. That was my first trip to Guam, and I was only there for two days, so I returned to Naha and received my 90 day visitor visa. For the first time, I was a tourist in Okinawa, with no sponsorship, and no contingency plan other than searching for a job that would sponsor me.

Meanwhile, I trained, and did odd jobs to make ends meet as my sparse savings quickly vanished. At the time, my wife had just begun working at a '*bento-ya*' (shop selling boxed lunches) near our apartment; one of the benefits to her job was that the staff were allowed to bring home the unsold bento at the end of their shift. This was literally a lifesaver as we would have had nothing to eat if it weren't for the kindness of Izumi's bosses. I can remember vividly having only rice, a small bottle of soy sauce, and two mackerel in the refrigerator on the day my wife started her new job. When she came home from work that first day with bags full of food, we were both overwhelmed with gratefulness; something that was taken for granted only months before, had now become precious. I can still remember what we had for dinner that night; Izumi had a simple *shio-yaki bento*, and I had *goya chanpuru bento*. As we were having dinner, my wife suggested that I apply for a spouse visa, until I could get job sponsorship, and we agreed that it was the best course of action for the time. After endless interviews with Japanese immigration officials, letters of reference from my landlord, and my father-in-law, I finally received a spouse visa, or *gaijin torokusho*. Now as a legal resident, I quickly found work as an apprentice block mason, and I soon found out two facts that were uniquely Japanese; one, kyuro-bi (payday) came once per month, and two, *zangyo* (overtime) just meant that we worked later, but we didn't get paid extra. Of course that explained all the strange looks from my coworkers as I asked if we would be working overtime. Maasa replied, "Yes, almost every day!" I was excited to hear this and replied, "*Joto* (very good)!" With payday a month away, and money being scarce, my good friend Mark Vickery, helped me with small loans and listened to me as we spoke about my new challenges; he invited us over for dinner quite often, and we enjoyed his Okinawan wife's delicious cooking. Not long after, Mark and Yuko moved back to America, and life slowly returned to normal as I began to feel at home with my Okinawan coworkers and friends.

Civilian Life

As a civilian expat living in Okinawa, life was certainly different than when I was an airman stationed at Kadena Air Base. My identity had changed from a temporary military resident to karate-man living in Okinawa. My language abilities in both *Nihongo* and *Uchinaguchi* expanded quite rapidly as I lived my daily life speaking barely any English at all. I received my honorable discharge from the United States Air Force in March 1994, and secured a visa and a translator/liaison contract with World Airways at the Kadena Air Base MAC terminal. The contract was short-lived as World Airways lost the "freedom bird" contract to FedEx, and I found myself scrambling to find work and sponsorship before my visa expired.

Through the introduction of a friend, I was hired as an apprentice block mason with CB Koei, and learned the job quickly. By the end of the summer, most of my American friends were gone; they had all left Okinawa due to PCS or had been discharged, and gone back home. Although I immersed myself daily with all things Okinawan, this was a lonely time in my life with no other daily American interaction. I found myself homesick for the first time in 5 years.

The author at work on a jobsite in Gushikawa, Okinawa. 1996

The work was physically demanding, and the hours were long, but the heavy lifting involved in masonry helped develop my physical strength and endurance, which, in turn, enhanced my karate. I learned to embrace my new life and made new friends with coworkers and peers from other *kaisha* (companies) as well. I went to work in the morning for an Okinawan construction company; I came home to my Okinawan wife, and I trained in the evenings at the Hamagawa Dojo. There were no other Americans at work, home, or the dojo, so I was experiencing the total-immersion method of learning a new language. Paying for utilities, buying groceries, buying gasoline, and dining out became part of my immersion experience. I only realized how immersed I had become when I spoke to my parents on the phone and became conscious of the fact that I was mixing Japanese and English during our conversation!

My wife and I hosted parties and barbeques at our small apartment in Chatan; Okinawan friends, family, and in-laws all spent time with us, and I dug deeper into the Okinawan culture. As time went on, I realized that the only Americans I associated with were those that shared my passion, or at least, those that were also married to Okinawans. I never really thought about why; I suppose it was just natural to be drawn to others who shared the same path, and the similar hardships that only we knew. There was a modicum of comfort and satisfaction in knowing and socializing with the other *gaijin* (foreigners) that perhaps shared the same emotions and perpetual homesickness. And while we were living in the tropical island paradise of Okinawa, there would always be sacrifices that only we knew.

Christmas Party at our home in Chatan, Okinawa. 1995

The author's In-laws and friends at our home in Chatan, Okinawa. 1995

Matsuri

Festivals are synonymous with Okinawa; the laid-back island life and mild year-round climate make Okinawa perfect for parties. From seasonal festivals, to *Obon* (festival to honor dead ancestors) *and Eisa* (traditional Okinawan dance used to pay respects and "wake" ancestors), there is always a reason to get together with friends and family to celebrate. A vital part of Okinawan longevity and happiness is attributed to frequent socialization and interaction with family, friends, and peers. In the winter (spring for Okinawa) families get together for *sakurami*, or Cherry Blossom Festival. In the summer, we have *Obon* and *Eisa* festivals, various music festivals, and the ever-popular Peaceful Love Rock Festival that always coincided with the *Orion Biru Matsuri*! Other festivals such as the *Tsuna-hiki* (giant tug-of-war) and *Naha Hari Matsuri* (Naha Port dragon-boat races) are popular with Okinawans and foreigners alike.

Masa-kun and Parker at Company Bonenkai: Urasoue, Okinawa 1995

Co-workers at the Company Bonenkai: Urasoue, Okinawa 1995

Karaoke time at the Company Bonenkai: Urasoue Okinawa 1995

Izumi (author's wife) at company beach party: Ginowan Okinawa 1996

For me, the best times always included close friends and family; the birthday parties, beach parties, karaoke nights, long dinner parties at the *Murasaki Izakaya* with my family and in-laws, and of course the company *Bonenkai* (Japanese end-of-year party; literally "forget the year").

Orion Beer Festival: Eisa Matsuri: Koza, Okinawa 1996

Taiko performers at the Eisa Matsuri: Koza, Okinawa 1996

These were the special times that made my experiences in Okinawa extraordinary. Through the friendships fostered and nurtured by a genuine passion for my hosts' culture and way of life, the Uchinanchu accepted me with open arms and made me feel like I was home.

Ichariba Chodee

In Okinawa, there is a very familiar saying: *Ichariba chodee* (when we meet, we are brothers, friends). This is truly the belief and culture of the Uchinanchu Okinawan people. This belief extends past their own culture and native people to the gaijin (foreigners) living on their beautiful island.

In my experience, the Okinawans are the friendliest people I have ever encountered. On several occasions, I was outside of my comfort zone of Kadena Air Base exploring the island. I would often stop and ask directions (in my elementary Japanese) to a shop or restaurant. Instead of simply answering my question, they almost always walked with me to my destination. Keep in mind, that I was a young 20-something American that they had never met—a perfect stranger—yet I was taken cheerfully to my destination. Ichariba chodee—When we meet, we are brothers.

Author and Jann Aki at the Columbus Dojo: 2002.

This culture of brotherhood and generosity very much encompasses Okinawan karate and its' practitioners. Over the years, I have had the opportunity to meet and train with so many wonderful people. It's always an instant connection—a brotherhood. After training and talking for an hour or two, it feels like we're a couple of old friends reconnecting. Many

L-R: Antonio Bustillo and the Author: Columbus Dojo, 2004.

of these friends, I only see every few years, some I see once a year—and with every reunion we pick up exactly where we left off as if we haven't missed a beat.

At the time of this writing, I am now in my third decade of practicing karate,

L-R: Michael Mitchell, Author (holding newborn son, Kenji), Antonio Bustillo: Columbus Dojo, 2004

and I feel very fortunate to have met so many other great practitioners. Some senior, some junior, all brothers and sisters. We share a common bond that unites us all in spirit, and as the months and years bring new opportunities to meet with more Okinawan karate practitioners, I happily welcome the chance to learn, train, and share. And above all, I am eager to meet my newest brothers and sisters in karate. To them, I say: Train hard, sweat buckets, listen intently, enjoy immensely. This is Okinawan Karate. Ichariba chodee!

Ganbatte!

When I lived in Okinawa, one of the first words that I learned (in the dojo) was *ganbatte*. This word was used by Takamiyagi Sensei; it was used by my senpai, and they said it a Lot! After a week or two, I began to think that my dojo nickname was "Ganbatte Pa-ka san!" Then... I finally checked one of my dictionaries for the translation of ganbatte: *do your best.*

In Okinawa, ganbatte is a term used by everyone... In the dojo, at sporting events, at concerts, among small children, from mothers to children before leaving for school in the morning. The concept of "ganbatte, doing your best" envelops the social culture of the people of Okinawa.

If you fail, ganbatte—try again and do your best. If you're nervous, ganbatte—reach deep down and do your best. This is the positive mental attitude that helps the Okinawans and Japanese succeed. Success requires tremendous effort and positive mental attitude. We must remember that *failure* is not the opposite of *success*; it is a part of success. When we attempt something difficult for the first time, and we fail, we must realize that the failure simply brings us one step closer to success!

Fall down? Get up and try again! Ganbatte!

Failure is frustrating and disheartening, and causes even the strongest to give up. You have the power to succeed! Remove "I can't" from your vocabulary. Infuse this positive mental attitude not only in the dojo, but in your daily life. You have the ability within you to accomplish things you haven't even imagined yet! Always do your best; never give up. Ganbatte!

The Sunabe Seawall

In 1993, my relationship with Takamiyagi Sensei began to evolve from that of student and teacher to the role of Sensei becoming a surrogate parent. Of course no one could ever replace my parents and the love, kindness, and nurturing that they so graciously provided; yet, in their absence my teacher began to fill the role. As a young man, I still needed advice on life issues, and Sensei was always nearby with an ear willing to listen.

One Saturday afternoon, I was cleaning the property around the dojo – a practice I had only recently started, due to my new understanding of *giri* (obligation or duty of the student). Takamiyagi Sensei arrived around noon, and we took a walk to the end of the block to the seawall in Sunabe to relax and enjoy the breeze. I honestly don't remember exactly what we talked about that day, but I do remember feeling very special because my teacher was spending time

Sunabe Seawall: near the Hamagawa Dojo in Chatan, Okinawa: 1991

talking to me outside of the dojo. Until that very day, I always presumed that he was unapproachable, and that it would be a breach of etiquette to socialize outside of the walls of the Hamagawa Dojo.

I was half-right. While we were spending time away from the dojo, it wasn't time spent socializing, as everything we spoke about was other lessons. Sensei would school me on the finer points of techniques, along with a generous portion of history lessons and even the occasional short story. He asked about my family and my life back in America, and he told me about his family, his life, and martial arts experiences. He spoke little of personal experiences, and indicative of his humble character, but he was very quick to praise his teachers and to share the impact they had on his development.

> These Saturday conversations at the seawall taught me so much about the proper mindset, behavior, and character of both a student and a teacher.

These Saturday conversations at the seawall taught me so much about the proper mindset, behavior, and character of both a student and a teacher. I learned to always give proper respect to my teachers, and to refrain from negativity and hurtful discussions when speaking of other teachers or systems.

Usually, we would sit for an hour or so, and then go up the street and around the corner to Hamaya Soba, a favorite local restaurant. We became regulars there, and after a couple of months, the waitress wouldn't wait for us to order. She knew that I would eat Okinawa soba and that Sensei would eat "Soki" Soba, so she brought the usual to our table within a couple of minutes. To me, that was a fantastic feeling of belonging and fitting in with the rest of the locals! When we ate lunch, there was usually very little conversation. We ate fairly quickly, and then we were on our way. (Those of you who have been to Okinawa or have eaten soba are probably grinning right now, because you know exactly what I mean).

Even though we weren't talking, the lessons didn't stop. I always observed the way that Takamiyagi Sensei interacted with other people; from the peers and friends that he encountered to the waitress, he always treated everyone with respect. He remained humble and polite, and through his actions, taught me to be the same.

Not Your Black Belt

One Friday evening after training, Takamiyagi Sensei called me to the side; *"Pa-ka, ashita... hima aru?* (Do you have free time tomorrow?)"

Sure, I told him, excited that I may get extra training on Saturday.

"Jo-to," he replied.

Sensei then proceeded to tell me that a few people were meeting in Koza near Nakanomachi (Koza's entertainment district, usually off-limits to foreigners) at 9 p.m. and I was expected to be there. "Don't drive," he exclaimed.

Hai Sensei, wakarimasu (I understand)." I wasn't sure exactly why I received an invitation to go out with my sensei and senpai for the first time, but I was thrilled nonetheless!

I met Sensei at our planned location, and was surprised that it was only Sensei, Naoki (Sensei's son, and my senpai), and Keida-san – another senpai. We walked past the "gaijin discos" Pyramid, 8-Beat, Apple House, and turned right toward the not very "gaijin friendly" area of Nakanomachi. We were met with scowls, stares, and glares from the middle-aged Okinawan patrons as we all graced the doors of the first establishment. I realized pretty quickly that I was the only foreigner in the place, and that they didn't welcome "my kind" there.

After Takamiyagi Sensei had a few words with the hostess, we were welcomed, and settled into a table for the evening. In a blink, we were served *tsukemono* (pickled vegetables), tofu with shaved *katsuo* (bonito fish), and *edamame* (soybeans in the pod); this was only seconds before a large bottle of *Kumisen Awamori* was brought to the table. As the night went on, we talked about karate, life, women... and the *Awamori* flowed. It seemed that everyone was focused on me; even when I tried to steer the conversation toward someone else, they quickly turned it back to me. Honestly, I didn't think anything of it; as an American who spoke Japanese, I had become accustomed to being a novelty amongst Okinawans. Eventually, the topic turned to the upcoming promotion test that was scheduled a few weeks from that night.

Sensei asked me if I thought I was ready for shodan.

I laughed it off, and said "No, Sensei. Not for a couple more years."

Sensei, said, "No, next month." I thought the *Awamori* was talking, so I asked him to repeat what he'd just said. He told me again, that I was expected to test for shodan the next month. I laughed again, thinking he was joking!

He looked at me sternly, and said, *"Honto dayo* (seriously, really)." I began to protest, partly because I knew that I wasn't ready, and partly because I thought that Sensei was administering some cruel test of my character and intentions. After a few minutes of going back and forth with him, he stopped and lowered his voice: "Pa-ka, why are rejecting my decision to test you? Do you think you know better than me if you're ready? Do you not trust my judgment?"

I was silent; the entire table went silent, as I slowly processed what I'd just heard. I realized quickly that I had just insulted my teacher by questioning his judgment. As my stomach started to churn and the lump in my throat grew larger, the only words that I could choke out were: *"Gomen nasai* (I'm sorry), Sensei."

Naoki had already refilled our glasses. Takamiyagi Sensei lowered his head slightly and peered over his glasses at me and said, *"Daijiyoubu Pa-ka. Kanpai!* (It's ok. Cheers!)" We lifted our glasses and finished our conversation and the Awamori.

The next morning, I rose early and contemplated everything that happened the night before; I didn't understand it all, but I was determined to break the gaijin stereotype, and be the best student I could possibly be.

The next few weeks flew by as I trained harder than ever before in preparation for my upcoming test. On test day, I thought I was going to vomit; I'd never been that nervous about anything in my entire life! I made it through, and was promoted to shodan that day in 1994, and although I was happy to have the ordeal finished, I didn't feel different at all. Later, as I was speaking to my senpai, Naoki mentioned something that brought extreme clarity to the late-night conversation with Takamiyagi Sensei the previous month in Nakanomachi. "Congratulations, now you work harder, Sensei will be proud of his new shodan!"

The author after Sho-dan promotion at the Hamagawa Dojo: Okinawa, 1995

That was it? Sensei's new shodan? So, after all the hard work, gallons of sweat, blood, broken fingers and toes, and bruises, it wasn't mine. It wasn't my black belt? No! It was Sensei's! Then it became clearer. A black belt is certainly a great goal, but every black belt is a reflection of the teacher. While the student works hard to earn the promotion – we would be nothing without our teacher to guide us along the way. So I realized a simple truth; we work hard, we train, and we sacrifice. A symbol of mastering the basics is the black belt promotion for the student, while the teacher is validated with every black belt student as well.

Kantoku

In 1995, when I was a new shodan, Takamiyagii Sensei asked me to work with a group of young students for the upcoming annual *Kodomo Karate Taikai* (children's karate tournament) held at the Okinawa Convention Center. I was given a group of six students to coach and tutor on the details of Er Shi Quan and Ta Jiao kata's from Goso Kenpo (Chinese Five Ancestor Boxing). This was a brand new experience for me, teaching by myself for the first time, and I was nervous that I wasn't qualified for the task. The weeks flew by quickly and I became more comfortable with my new role of coaching the children; I was actually excited when the big day came. We met at the dojo early on a Saturday morning and loaded up in the van to head to the Ginowan Convention Center. Sensei lectured the children about respect, behavior, and told them to do their best.

We all filed into the venue, and Sensei spoke briefly to the organizers to get everyone registered. The kids were looking around (as I was) mesmerized by the thousands of young karate students accompanied by their teachers. There were representatives from every *ryu* (style) of karate on the island, and nearly every dojo; according to the program there were 132 different dojo represented. There were famous faces in the crowd and on the floor, Nakazato Sensei, Yagi Sensei, Nakamura Sensei, the Shinjo brothers, Sakumoto,

144	極心館 天願チーム	セイサン	天願太地・佐渡山司・金城健一郎	高江洲武隼
145	上地流屋富祖 修武館Aチーム	完　周	久場晶博・大城塁史・喜屋武克人	高江洲義裕
146	洗 心 館 Ｅ	普及型Ｉ	井口譲・屋比久優季・吉田正輝	津波政宏
147	明武館豊見城 道場Aチーム	撃砕第二	運天泰治・川村祐也・兼浜洋平	諸喜田猛
148	大 城 道 場 Ｂ チ ー ム	ナイハンチ初段	照屋勇也・具志堅将吾・久貝政貴	宮城正一
149	武道館Ｂチーム	セイサン	金城優介・仲村渠馨也・仲村渠博人・照屋毅紀	宮里幸市
150	南風原修武館 Ｂ チ ー ム	完 子 和	照喜名邦彦・宮城弘樹・長元洋	島袋春吉
151	翁 長 道 場	ピンアン二段	山城文乃・上間達也・金城愛	新里かおり
152	儀 保 道 場 Ｂ チ ー ム	ナイハンチ初段	座安弘隆・本村雄一・糸数恭太	知念　勝
153	糸満市スポーツ 少 年 団 Ｎ	サイファー	玉城陽香・新垣安希恵・玉城幸訓	玉城幸雄
154	五首館Ｃチーム	二 十 拳	饒平名知行・山田義康・平良勝也	ゲアリー・バーカー
155	久場川同心会	完 子 和	砂川正人・仲里仁貴・大浜義得	亀井里加
156	洗 心 館 Ｆ	アーナンクー	花城雄太・徳吉広一・平良旦	平良　滋
157	志喜館比嘉空手 道場屋良チーム	ピンアン初段	屋良直輝・伊佐義晃・翁長正保	比嘉　司
158	剛勇館新城道場	制 引 戦	久高誉士朗・与那嶺良太・東太田馨	渡久山洋樹
159	兼城修武館	完　周	新垣修作・新崎長慎・新崎佑悟	儀間清久
160	上運天４組	ナイハンチ初段	与那嶺徹弥・大城友輝・諸喜田二光	田港朝史

Hokama, and dozens of lesser known karate masters all filled the competition floor with their students. After we checked in and got the schedule, Sensei informed us that we had a couple of hours before our teams were up, so we had time to practice, mingle, and look around. I took the opportunity to walk around and was pleased to find another American in a *gi* (karate uniform); we spoke for a few minutes about training and then went our separate ways.

As I made my way around the floor, several folks stopped to chat for a minute or two; apparently, I was one of only a few foreigners out the thousands in attendance that day, so naturally, the Okinawans were curious about me and wondered who was my teacher. Most were disappointed when they found out I was no-one they had ever heard of, and some even questioned why I was there as only a *shodan*. I had no answer other than: my Sensei had asked me to help, so I did. I quickly realized that I was in the minority as a young man with a new shodan. Most other *kantoku* (coaches) were at least three-dan or above. Suddenly I felt extremely unworthy of the task I had accepted from Sensei; I quickly realized I was a tiny fish in the great big pond of karate… but I was determined to take the task seriously and ensure that my best effort was issued. So, I rounded up my team of kids and we went outside to practice. The looks we got from the other Okinawans were unforgettable; we must have seemed quite out of place, a young American leading a group of Okinawan kids in Chinese kata practice. That day, we didn't win any medals, but it was ok, I had a great time, learned a lot, represented my Sensei and our dojo well, and received a new title: *kantoku* or coach. It had a nice ring to it.

Every Day Is a Test

In January 1994, I finalized my separation paperwork and started my 63 days of terminal leave; I had already secured employment and was excited about my new freedom that came with civilian life. I had already spoken to Takamiyagi Sensei about my plans to separate from the Air Force and remain on the island to live and train. I was confident that he would be thrilled at my dedication to stay in Okinawa to train, after all, how many students would give up a free trip home after living overseas for years, right? Wrong. After I expressed my intention and shared my goals, Sensei looked at me, and said, "Go home."

Wait, did I misunderstand? My Japanese language skills were a work in progress, so I was sure that I misunderstood or maybe I misinterpreted what Sensei had just said. I asked him to repeat what he'd just told me.

He was clearer the second time: *"Nande America ni kaerimasen-ka? Kaeru houga ii dayo* (Why aren't you going back to America? It's better if you go back.)" It was crystal clear that time, I was more than disappointed. I'd already decided that I was staying in Okinawa, and had made arrangements to give up my free ticket home as I prepared for the next chapter of my life. The request for separation on the island had already been approved by my commander, I had already secured contract employment as an interpreter and night operations co-manager for the World Airways terminal on Kadena Air Base, and had actually already started my new job while on terminal leave.

I explained to Sensei that I had already decided to stay, and there was no changing my mind. He said: *"Jaa… ganbatte Pa-ka san* (Do your best, Parker.)"

After a month or so, I approached Takamiyagi Sensei about advising me as I started my search for an apartment; with only a month left in the barracks, it was time to find a place of my own.

Sensei agreed to help, and told me to meet him at the dojo early Saturday morning. We met, and Sensei drove me around to look at half a dozen apartments in my price range, although some of them were a little out of the way and in different towns. I wanted a place in Sunabe or Chatan that was close to the dojo, but Sensei started out in Koza and then Okinawa City, and on to Yomitan before finally showing me a third floor apartment in Chatan that was near Kadena's Gate 1, and within walking distance of the dojo. The Chatan apartment wasn't the nicest, or cheapest, but it was the right location, so that was the one I chose. I signed the lease and moved in a few weeks later. Life went on as I worked, trained, and enjoyed life! Several months passed, and I invited Sensei and some of my dojo senpai to my apartment for a summer BBQ. As we ate, drank, and talked, Sensei asked how I liked the apartment. I told him that I liked it just fine as it was close to the dojo, then I asked why he showed me the other apartments so far away from the dojo before he showed me the one that I was now leasing. This had puzzled me since that Saturday in February when we went apartment hunting, and his answer puzzled me even more, although in hindsight, the answer he gave was perfectly clear. Sensei was testing me... making sure that I was staying in Okinawa for the reason that I had told him; to continue my training.

I learned another lesson that day; every day is a test.

Chuura Umi

The beautiful sea. This really sums up the vision of Okinawa. Whether you have ever trained in karate or not, a spectacular part of the Okinawan culture and way of life revolves around the beautiful sea! From the shipyards of Naha and Tomari, to the fishing docks scatter along the shores of the island, Okinawa is now, as it was in centuries past, dependent on the bounty of the sea. Early in the morning, during low tide, I would go to my favorite spot in Sunabe to gather clams and sea grapes along with the dozens of Okinawans that were doing the same. Weekends spent snorkeling, scuba diving, and fishing for *gurugun* (native fish) helped pass the time while exposing me to a piece of Okinawa's culture that most Okinawans live, and many foreigners miss. Of course there are dozens of dive shops in Chatan, and hundreds of Americans and foreign tourists come to get PADI (scuba) certification, and dive the reefs just beyond the Sunabe seawall, but this is the tourist side. The reef there has literally been trampled to death, with little activity of sea life due to heavy human traffic.

I learned early on, that to experience the "real Okinawa," go where the locals go. Venture out to the places with no foreigners, no English language signs, (or no signs at all) and just observe. There is spot that I used to dive often near Onna Village, with an enormous cluster of brain coral as large as two houses. The sea life that lived on that one cluster was more vibrant and unique than anything I'd ever seen. There was no sign, no parking lot, and the road to the rocky beach was nearly unnavigable. From time to time, I would see an *Ojisan* or *Obasan* (old man or woman) wading out with nets to fish, but no other divers or snorkelers. This became my private oasis for those rare occasions when I wanted to get away from the hustle and bustle of my daily life. I could stay all day, from sunrise to sunset, and rarely see another human being. With nothing but the beautiful sea, the sun glistening off the water as the waves lapped the shoreline, and the serenade of the native birds as they flew over looking for dinner, I was at peace; I felt one with nature, and I felt a connection to the ancestral Uchinanchuu who undoubtedly fished these same waters in centuries past. I often found myself wondering how much karate was practiced on this small secluded beach under the moonlight. I wondered as I looked at the rocky beach, how much *bojutsu* (staff fighting) or *ekujutsu* (oar fighting) may have been practiced, or how many refinements were discovered in utilizing the *suna-kake* waza (sand throwing technique) with such unorthodox mixture of sand and pebbles on this beach. I smiled with satisfaction as I thought how many thousands of Uchinanchuu had found their personal peace with this view of the beautiful sea.

Okinawa Time

Everyone that has spent any amount of time in Okinawa knows the term "Okinawa time." The combination of the tropical island life, friendly happy people, and rich cultural farming and fishing roots, all blend together to form a laid-back culture: the Okinawan people take their time. For the most part, no one is in a rush; there isn't much hustle and bustle on the island, and people really take their time to enjoy the little treasures of island life.

Karate training is pursued with the same approach. There is no rush to learn the next kata or earn the next promotion. I can't even remember the children in the dojo asking about their next belt color. On the contrary, everyone was happy to be where they were, simply enjoying life, enjoying training, and taking their time on the journey. Are things different in Okinawa than America because everyone knows that karate will always be around? Perhaps so. If we had literally hundreds of legitimate highly skilled, and experienced karate masters within a few square miles, would our approach be less hurried? Regardless of your answer, I feel that we can, and should learn from the Okinawan approach to life and Karate. Slow down, take your time, and enjoy the journey.

In Okinawa, I became a man. After a year in Korea, I arrived in Okinawa as a fresh-faced young airman ready for my next assignment; years later, as a veteran with a new wife and kids in tow, we prepared for our next great adventure in the United States; In September 1996, we sold most of what we owned, packed our clothes along with a few mementos, and headed West.

CHAPTER 2

Home Again

Culture Shock

It was nearly midnight as we made our way to Delta's luggage area; the long flight from Okinawa had drained my wife and me, and our three children were cranky and sleepy, still wondering what was going on. I located our bags, and we began trudging toward the entrance of the Atlanta Hartsfield Airport when I looked up and saw two familiar silhouettes walking faster and then running toward us. My parents had come to pick us up at the airport and drive my family and I back to Columbus, Georgia. After not seeing each other for nearly six years, we embraced for what seemed like minutes. My mother was hugging my wife and her grandchildren, whom she had just met for the first time, and was quite an emotional sight! As we loaded the family into my parents' van for the long drive home, I couldn't help but feel a little strange... somewhat out of place, but I couldn't quite put my finger on it. While my father was driving and we were chatting, I realized that he was driving on the wrong side of the road. In Korea and Okinawa, I had become accustomed to driving on the left side, and although I had driven on the right side in America for a few years prior to being stationed in Asia, it no longer felt correct. Over the next few months, I adjusted to life in America, and overcame my mild case of culture shock. The driving was the easiest part to overcome; being landlocked and not having access to the ocean, beaches, and fresh seafood (think sushi) was very difficult for both my wife and me.

After a couple of weeks, we were settled into our new apartment, and I decided that I'd had a long enough break from training, so I picked up a phone book and compiled a list of all the "karate schools" in the area. I visited

> I compiled a list of all the "karate schools" in the area. I visited each one, and quickly realized that I was a long way from home.

each one, and quickly realized that I was a long way from home. The schools here were absolutely nothing like the dojo in Okinawa. Some were a little misleading; I checked out two different 'karate' schools that taught Tae Kwon Do (Korean martial art). The first one I visited, explained to me that karate is a more recognizable word than Tae Kwon Do, and there were fewer letters, so the signage was cheaper! I thanked him and left.

One place that actually claimed a link to Okinawan karate was quite different when I visited in person. The teacher was polite and sincere, but the giant airbrushed dragon on the dojo wall coupled with the fact that he insisted on being addressed as "grandmaster" just didn't do it for me. I was in disbelief. Is this what karate looks like in America? This 'dojo' had a wall full of trophies, but not a single makiwara on the wall, no hojo undo equipment, nothing that would identify this place as an Okinawan karate dojo. My culture shock was in high gear, and I was ready to get my family and board the next flight out to Okinawa. Looking back, I suppose that I was rather sheltered coming back to America; after all, the only karate I had ever known, and all that I had been taught was while living in Okinawa – the literal cradle of karate – and how can anyone realistically compare to that unless they had traveled the same path?

A New Chapter

The karate landscape in Columbus wasn't looking any prettier, so I trained solo. I practiced *kihon* (basic techniques), I practiced *kata* (forms), I practiced makiwara and iron shirt/iron body, but something was missing. I didn't have training partners to push me; I didn't have my senpai to encourage and challenge me, and most importantly, I didn't have a teacher to guide me. After a year in the apartment, we moved into a much larger house with a spacious

Construction of the original Goshukan-Ryu Columbus Dojo: Columbus, Georgia, 1998

backyard that we felt was the perfect place to raise a family. I continued training at the new house, and the weeks turned into months. Summer 1998 was approaching, and along with the summer months came blazing-hot temperatures and the promise of a harsher, wetter environment for my open-air backyard training in the grass. After talking it over with my wife, I began construction on a private dojo in our backyard. It was nothing fancy, just an old-fashioned wood-framed dojo with a lean-to roof, a few windows, a few lights, and a wooden floor. The design was modeled after Sensei's Hamagawa Dojo in Okinawa, and was built purely for functionality.

I built in stages as funds became available. First was the floor, a 16'x32' deck that sat about a foot off the ground, which was my dojo until late August when I finally put up the walls and roof.

Garry Parker inside the original Columbus Dojo: Columbus, Georgia 1999

For the next couple months, I had a perfect open-air dojo. The shade of a large Georgia pine tree kept the temperature bearable, while the open walls allowed

an occasional breeze to blow through. As winter approached, I wrapped the frame in thick industrial plastic and, with the aid of two space heaters, the dojo was quite comfortable for training all season. Spring came quickly; the plastic was peeled off and the open-air training was a welcome relief.

I had a nicely equipped dojo at that point: a few heavy bags, pads, some mats, a very nice makiwara collection, *hojo undo* equipment, and even a mirror on the wall. But something was still missing. I felt lonely in the dojo, I felt stagnant; although I practiced daily, I was certain that I was not growing in skill.

Frustrated, I called my Sensei, and told him of my dilemma. I explained that although I was keeping up my training, I felt no growth. I needed interaction, feedback, correction, and most of all, I needed my Sensei. I went on to tell him that my wife and I had discussed it, and were ready to move back to Okinawa. She would be happier around her family and friends, and I would be happier being back in Sensei's dojo. As I paused and waited for Sensei to tell me what a great idea it was, and how much he wanted to see me back in the dojo, I was rattled (once again) by his response. "No. You stay in America. You have dojo, ne?"

"Hai Sensei, but it's small, and it's in my backyard, and it's just for me, and I don't have a teacher here!"

"*Daijiyoubu, Pa-ka san*, you teach."

I objected; we'd been down this road before. Sensei told me I was ready for something, I objected, he scolded me for questioning his judgment, and he won. Still, I objected again. I know the rules in Okinawa. I didn't meet the grade requirements, nor did I have a *menjo* (license to teach) and I reminded him of that.

Sensei interjected, "No, you teach family and a few friends, and then you learn more."

I objected for the third time. "I don't know how to teach, Sensei."

"Teach kihon, teach Naihanchi, but always kihon." He went on to explain that I simply needed to teach kihon and a couple of kata, and come to Okinawa periodically to train and learn new kata and new skills. The rest would take care of itself. Reluctantly, I agreed, and in March 1999, I officially opened the first Okinawa Goshukan-Ryu branch dojo in America… in my backyard with my wife, my brother-in-law, and one coworker as students.

Breaking New Ground

After I began teaching, I started networking and found a few more karateka that, like me, were hidden from the mainstream and couldn't be found in the Yellow Pages. Although we trained in different *ryu-ha* (styles), we had enough in common to learn from each other. Long before karate was systemized into specific styles, teachers came together to train, share, and research. Everyone learned from each other and the result was historical. In that spirit, I created the first "Goshukan Gasshuku," a weekend of like-minded traditional martial artists training, sharing, and learning from one other. Over the years, I have met some outstanding men and women, talented teachers, and people that have become very close friends. We are separated only by time and distance, and every year that we get together for the Gasshuku, it's like a big family reunion!

Everyone should take the time and opportunity to attend seminars, workshops, training camps, karate clinics, and Gasshuku whenever possible. The benefit of these events are multi-faceted: First, you meet new people and make new friends; second, you find out that your style isn't the only one nor is it the best one; and third, you may even find out that you can learn something new, if you walk in with an open mind.

Keys to the Kingdom

In December 2003, my wife was pregnant with our youngest child, Kenji; while Izumi stayed home in Georgia, I went back to Okinawa for a few weeks to train and visit family and friends. Because I was alone, Sensei offered to let me stay at the (then new) *honbu* (headquarters) dojo; he had a full bathroom with shower and a futon in the corner of the office... What more could I ask for!

I arrived on a late flight, met by my friend and fellow USAF vet James, who picked me up at the airport and drove me to the hotel. I had decided to wait until the next day to meet my Sensei, as it was late and I didn't want to bother him. The next morning after I woke and had breakfast, Sensei picked me up and drove me to the dojo. This was the first time I had seen the new dojo as it was only built the previous year, so I was really excited to see it.

Takamiyagi Hiroshi at the entrance of the New Okinawa Goshukan-Ryu Honbu Dojo: Okinawa 2002

As Sensei gave me the tour, I noticed that although the building was brand new, it still had the same layout and the same feel. No drastic changes had been made other than the presence of air conditioners, which were still wrapped in the original plastic, and to my knowledge, Sensei still hasn't plugged them in and turned them on.

The *shomen* (ancestral shrine), the dressing room, and even Sensei's office was all still in the same place as in the old dojo. The only modification in layout was that the makiwara had all been relocated a little farther down the wall.

The brand-new honbu dojo still felt like home. We trained for a

New Okinawa Goshukan-Ryu Honbu Dojo 2003. L-R: Takamiyagi Naoki, Takamiyagi Hiroshi, Garry Parker.

couple hours (meaning I demonstrated kata and received corrections for a couple of hours) and then took a lunch break around noon. It was our old favorite soba restaurant a couple of blocks from the dojo... ahh, just like old times!

After lunch we went to the Sunabe seawall and chatted for a while, primarily about my family, and a little about my students too. We returned to the dojo to train some more, and after an hour or so, Sensei told me to get some rest because he would be back in a few hours to pick me up for a "little party." Before he left, Sensei gave me two keys: one for the front door of the dojo, and one for the office. He reminded me to lock the door when I left, and was on his way.

To most people, this was an insignificant thing, a meaningless gesture. To me, it meant that Sensei trusted me without question; he trusted my character and he trusted my judgment. Not once did he give instructions or rules for staying in the dojo. To me, that meant I had gained not only his trust, but his respect as well.

Some people would likely feel more comfortable in a hotel room with a full bed, television, and air conditioning, but not me. I had been given the keys to the kingdom.

Over the next couple weeks, I settled into a routine of waking up at dawn, walking down the street to watch the sunrise in the cool morning air, then back to the dojo to train for a couple hours before breakfast. I left the lights off and trained in the shadows with only the morning sunlight slowly drifting through the windows. When the dojo was fully illuminated by the morning sun, it was time to shower and go to a late breakfast before my daily activities. When Sensei arrived around noon, I received one-on-one instruction that I'll forever cherish, but there was something so peaceful, so surreal, about training solo in the quiet darkness of the early morning. No sounds other than the squeak of my feet on the floor as I stepped and pivoted, the rustle of my gi as I moved by body in kata, the snap of the makiwara with every strike, and my breath, both audible and visible, on those cool December mornings.

In Okinawa, I became a man. After a year in Korea, I arrived in Okinawa as a fresh-faced young airman ready for my next assignment. Years later, as a veteran with a new wife and kids in town, we prepared for our next great adventure in the United States. In September 1996, we sold most of what we owned, packed our clothes along with a few mementos, and headed west.

CHAPTER 3

Kazoku Dojo

Kazoku: family. With only a few years' teaching experience, I could think of nothing better than being surrounded by my family in the dojo. It was March 1999, and I had been authorized to open the first Goshukan-ryu branch dojo in America. Having my family and a few friends for my first students helped ease the nervousness I felt every time I bowed in with the class; still it was an odd feeling. For the past 15 years I had been perfectly content to line up, bow in, and train hard. Now I found myself standing in front of a handful of people in this tiny backyard dojo; they were all people that I knew and loved, and they were eager to learn, but it may as well have been 100 strangers standing in front of me.

Eventually, I became more comfortable with my new role, but it was a slow process. Without the loving support of my family–specifically my wife and children–I'm uncertain if I would have continued teaching. The truth is, I found such joy in every small improvement from my students, and that – along with my sense of duty to my Sensei – is really what kept me going. This entire chapter is dedicated to kazok –my family. In addition to my wife and children, other neighborhood children and children of family friends came to train with us in those first few years. These students all became part of our extended dojo family; we laughed and struggled, shared joys and pains together, and with such a tight-knit support system, even the largest challenges seemed to shrink.

Izumi and the Parker children inside the Columbus Dojo: Winter 1999.

Kazoku Dojo   43

I would like to share some of my greatest memories in the pages that follow. You'll see photos of my wife and young children, along with other members of our dojo family. The photos span several years, so you will also be able to see the dojo transformation as well.

The author with his children inside the Columbus Dojo: Winter 1999. Notice the plastic sheeting around the walls as the exterior paneling wasn't yet installed.

Spring 2000. Private family training on Saturday morning. Some of the exterior paneling has been installed and most of the plastic siding has been removed.

Spring 2000. Private family training on Saturday morning. Some of the exterior paneling has been installed and most of the plastic siding has been removed.

Winter 2000, Izumi and the Parker girls in the dojo.

The humble beginnings in our original backyard dojo set the bar for everything to come. Although we outgrew this dojo, and moved into a larger one in 2005, the five years in that "sweatbox" dojo helped shape and mold some fantastic karateka. In an era where 45 minute classes, juice bars, and

Early Spring 2001, Columbus Dojo Entrance. Exterior paneling has been completed, and new 'tou machiwara' has been installed.

Spring 2003- new mats installed and floors refinished at Columbus Dojo.

Okinawa Goshukan-Ryu Columbus Dojo: 2004

Okinawa Goshukan-Ryu Columbus Dojo: 2004

parents coaching from the sidelines had become the norm in other martial arts schools, we had a handful of adults and a dozen kids–mostly girls–that trained hard, sweated profusely in our old-fashioned dojo with one fan and no air-conditioning, and they did it all with smiles on their faces!

These were the hard and proven methods I learned from the time I tied on my first white belt as a high school student, until I tied on my first black belt

Okinawa Goshukan-Ryu Columbus Dojo: 2004

in Okinawa 11 years later. My students were exposed to the same type of old-school training that helped develop and mold me as a teen and young adult. They never complained; in fact, they all seemed to embrace the hard training. For most, it was their first experience in a dojo, so anything they learned was new and presumed to be the correct way to train. It was the same for me, too. It wasn't until I had a dojo of my own that I discovered that everyone didn't train with the same intensity as we did in Okinawa. It was absolutely shocking to me.

> It wasn't until I had a dojo of my own that I discovered that everyone didn't train with the same intensity as we did in Okinawa. It was absolutely shocking to me.

The bond that was created between me and a handful of students in those early years has been carried on. Although the dojo has grown and changed locations several times over the years, we are still that tight-knit and caring family of karateka that we were in that little backyard dojo. As new students come into the dojo, they are quickly taken under the wing of a senior, and that senior fills the role of big brother/

sister to help the new students acclimate to the culture of a family-type bond within the dojo. As a teacher, I look at my students as my karate 'children' and I feel a deep responsibility to guide them, advise them, get to know them and trust them so that we can have the proper student-teacher relationship. In my opinion, it is only through this type of bond that a student can trust and be trusted enough to reach their full potential as a karateka.

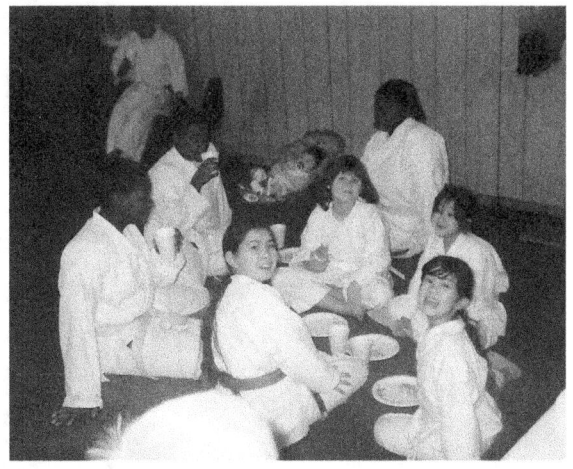

Winter 2004, Dojo Christmas Party.

In the years since then, I've observed how others train. In the following chapter, details, principles, and methods of training are described from both the student and teacher viewpoints.

BOOK TWO
LESSONS

CHAPTER 4

Training

"When you train, do so as if on the battlefield. Your eyes should glare, shoulders drop, and body harden. You should always train with intensity and spirit as if actually facing the enemy, and in this way you will naturally be ready."
—Itosu Ankoh, 1908

Train Anyway

We train when we feel like training. We train when our schedule tells us it's time to train. We train harder for upcoming events, tests, seminars, and training camps. This is fairly standard among the majority of martial artists, would you agree? Here's something else that is becoming prevalent among martial artists: excuses.

Takamiyagi Hiroshi Hanshi – teaching at the Goshukan Honbu Dojo in Okinawa. 2002

Partner drills and karate practice at the Goshukan Honbu Dojo in Okinawa. 2002

Invalid excuses that martial artists utter never cease to surprise me, and over the past 15 years teaching at the Columbus Dojo, I've heard a wide variety of them:

- I'm tired/I overslept.
- I forgot to wash/dry my gi.
- My foot/ankle/wrist/leg/arm hurts.
- I had a bad day at work/school.
- I'm sad/depressed/angry/anxious.
- I have a sunburn/headache/pimple on my nose.
- I had an argument with my wife/husband/boyfriend/girlfriend and I was in a bad mood.

As ridiculous as they sound, they are all real and genuine. These are the most common excuses that I've heard over the years. Are they valid reasons to excuse training? In my opinion, no. These are simply an exhibition of the students' priorities. If you decide to make consistent training a priority, then you will consistently train. It's that simple.

Kata practice at the Goshukan Honbu Dojo in Okinawa - 2003. Takamiyagi Naoki Sensei (L) Shoya-san (R)

This extends to training in the dojo as well. When we come to the dojo, we come to train. When you are on the floor wearing your gi, you are there to train, period. No excuses. No quitting when you feel uncomfortable. No stepping off the mats when you're out of breath. Train harder, train consistently, and reward yourself with the pride of knowing that you didn't give in to excuses.

I want to assure you that I, like you, have a real life outside of the dojo; I have stress, pressure, family, work, and health issues just as you do. I am not immune to the ups and downs of life, nor do I feel like training every single time you see me at the dojo. But no matter what I have going on — with the exception of unavoidable circumstances including illness and injury — I go to the dojo, and train anyway.

No matter what excuse you think you have, training will only yield positive results. Get your gi on, throw your excuses away, and train anyway.

> No matter what excuse you think you have, training will only yield positive results; get your gi on, throw your excuses away, and train anyway.

Do vs. Jutsu

To the initiated, many of the terms and some of the content of this section will be familiar; to the uninitiated, I will attempt to describe the fundamentals in simple terms.

Most classical (Asian) martial artists are familiar with the terms karate-do, budo, judo, kendo, iaido, and their counterparts karate-jutsu, bujutsu, jujutsu, kenjutsu, nand iaidutsu, and the like. How many are familiar with the background and meaning of the terms, how the different suffix changes their meaning, and the associated kanji that define them?

We'll start with the reading of the kanji for *Do,* also read as *Michi.*

The common meaning for Do is: way, path, or road. So, when we describe karate-do, we are describing the way or the path to practice karate. To many people, this way of practice is very literal, as the training is about the journey down the path of karate; a journey of attaining personal enlightenment, achieving inner peace and balance. This journey is what we as teachers will use to help guide our students on the path of personal improvement and higher character. We practice karate-do in order to achieve personal improvement and a higher self-understanding, and even the kata that we consistently practice may take on a zen-like aura of moving meditation when we let go of mental distraction and become tuned to our physiological movements.

Now that the "way" of karate has been described and defined, let's move on to the "why" of karate.

Jutsu is the practical application, the execution, or the tactics of a particular movement or art form. We are familiar with jujutsu (the soft/pliable art) and perhaps kenjutsu (sword arts); how many are familiar with: s*hujutsu* (surgery) or *senjutsu* (tactical strategy)? How about *gijutsu* (techniques) or g*oshinjutsu* (the art of self-defense)?

The common element in each one of these terms is that jutsu implies the practical, tactical application or implementation of each accompanying field of study. For example: *shujutsu* is the act of a surgical operation, while a medical student may study *shudo-bunkai* (the study of surgical process). A medical student that studies the process may not ever perform the act of surgery, depending on his or her medical specialty. However, we will certainly never see a surgeon that is untrained in the study and details of the surgical procedure in which he specializes.

According to the associated kanji of the suffixes *do* and *jutsu*, we can be confident that while karate-do is the philosophical *study* of the way/path of karate, karate-jutsu is the *practice* of the tactical implementation and practical application of karate. So, which is correct? Which one should we study? The answer simply is: both. The study of karate-jutsu without the study of karate-do is incomplete, and vice-versa.

> We practice karate-do in order to achieve personal improvement and a higher self-understanding...

To remain effective, we should train so that we are able to effortlessly and instinctively use our skills for protection. This isn't going to happen only from kata practice, makiwara punching, bag/padwork, ippon kumite (one-step sparring), renzoku kumite (continuous fighting), or jiyuu kumite (free fighting). The jutsu instinct can only be developed by constant high-stress, high-speed training that closely mimics the pressure and danger of a real assault. One earmark of the jutsu training is a warrior mindset: your enemy versus you. Only one can survive. When we train with this in mind, one of our most dangerous enemies is defeated—the enemy of self-doubt. A warrior isn't fearless. A warrior isn't invincible. A warrior is confident in the skills that have been developed through hard training, and is not willing to accept defeat.

We can summarize that the study of Do (the way) will help keep us morally grounded, civilized, and balanced with the proper mindset to make the correct decision when the time comes to practice the jutsu (tactical application) that ensures our safety and survival. Keep in mind that the difference between the practice of do and jutsu is often age, intent, and experience.

This isn't intended to imply a lesson plan, nor a judgmental assessment of the way others train; it's simply my viewpoint based on training coupled with real-life experiences. If you have questions regarding this subject, please ask your teacher first.

Train as if your life depends on it because someday it may.

Challenge Your Comfort Zone

2013 was full of changes for me, and with each change came the challenge of adapting and succeeding at each one. In January, I returned to college. In July, I began the study of iaido (the way of sword drawing).

As a middle-aged man with the responsibilities of family, career, training and teaching martial arts, returning to college was a big decision—but an easy one. A dynamic shift in time management was required to accommodate my class and homework schedule, and within a couple of months, I adapted. This was my third time in college; the first two were mildly interesting, but primarily a chore. Returning to college to pursue the next level of education at my age honestly concerned me. I questioned whether I could be open-minded enough to learn new information, and I've been pleasantly surprised. I actually enjoyed my formal education experience as a middle-aged man.

A longtime interest of mine has been the Japanese *bugei* or the art of the sword. Kenjutsu, Iaijutsu and Iaihyodo (Japanese sword arts) have always been out of my reach due to an unavailability of a qualified local teacher. Recently, I was given the opportunity to begin the study and practice of Mugai-ryu Iaido through a good friend and fellow karate teacher, Ron Davis. For more than 30 years, I have trained and practiced the empty-handed fighting arts. I thought that after all my years of experience fighting with hands, feet, and limbs that picking up a *bokken* (wooden training sword) or *katana* (metal sword) would be a simple transition. I was wrong. The movements are very surgical and precise in comparison to Okinawan karate, which is based on internal power generation, physical conditioning,

> We have the power to change, to climb higher, to do more... this requires us to get out of our comfort zone, challenge ourselves, and sacrifice...

and principles of movement. Both arts share the concept of *ma-ai* (proper distancing) and timing. For me, it has been quite a challenge adapting to this new art—a challenge that I fully embrace.

As we settle into our comfort zones, it's extremely easy to become stagnant; sometimes, it sneaks up on us. However, we—you and I—have the power to change, to climb higher, to do more, and sometimes—no, most of the time—this requires us to get out of our comfort zones, challenge ourselves, and sacrifice a little more.

> There are many paths to the same summit of enlightenment. Some travelers blast straight up hard and fast; others take the scenic route.

Do it for your family or do it for yourself; find a reason and do it.

Your Own Path

We previously spoke of karate-do, or the way/path of karate. Here we'll discuss further details of this path.

For you (the reader) and me (the writer), our journey on the *path of karate* has only one distinctive similarity; we must take the very first step in order to begin our journey. Many have taken that first step of enrolling in the dojo, training, learning, and practicing. Many leave the path quickly, some stay a while, and even others continue their journey until their dying breath.

For some, the path will be straight and steep, with the traveler trudging constantly forward to reach the summit. Others may encounter rocky paths along their journey. They will have setbacks, or breaks in training due to illness, injury, or other life circumstances. They may have to sit and rest, and then they return to the path—still they trudge forward. Others may start on the path with no problems, only to get lost along the way. Their focus may have blurred for any number of reasons. Perhaps they got distracted by ego, popularity, or chasing rank instead of knowledge. Any of these will cause the traveler to lose sight of the goal, and get lost on the path. Friends and students: it isn't important that your path and my path are the same; there are many paths to the same summit of enlightenment. Some travelers blast straight up hard and fast; others take the scenic route. Both paths are good; both offer personal rewards, challenges, and obstacles.

> Don't compare yourself to others on the path of budo. Find your own path, and be happy.

We all have different aspirations, goals, and thoughts of what our summit should be. We want enlightenment, health, life protection skills, balance, and a sense of accomplishment. Don't compare yourself to others on the path of budo. Find your own path, and be happy. How you get to the summit is not as important as staying on the path. Above all, enjoy the journey my friends!

Playing Karate

Most of us are familiar with competitive sports; we grew up playing football, baseball, basketball, hockey, and soccer. This type of playing is centered on competition, and victory is the ultimate goal. The player's days and weekends are filled with countless hours of training, conditioning and drills in preparation for an hour or so on the field, court, or ice rink... and dreaming of victory. The average part-time amateur athlete will train at least 4-6 hours per week.

Now, I am not going in the direction that many readers might expect with this topic. This is not about competition training. Read on.

Checkers, monopoly, charades... these are also games that many of us have played throughout childhood, and even well into adulthood. This is a different type of playing; it is for leisure, fun, or even a little friendly competition. The games are simple and easy to learn, and require little to no practice to maintain skill. One can go without practice for months or years and still play these games comfortably.

Personally, I haven't played checkers in years; but put a board in front of me, though, and I'll be as confident as the last time I played. Many karate students take this same approach regarding their training. Although we offer every student the opportunity to train three days per week in the dojo, some are completely satisfied if they attend class only once a week. These same students usually will not make the time to practice away from the dojo... and it shows.

But it's ok, they're only playing karate, right? No, not necessarily; they're busy working or studying, or they're tired (again), or sick, or it's bad weather… you get the picture.

To be clear, I believe that training once per week is much more beneficial than not training at all!

I also believe very sincerely that all valuable pursuits are worth some sacrifice. Constant improvement in my skill, character, and health are developed through consistent training. This requires sacrificing my time, comfort, and sometimes money. For me, these sacrifices are actually an investment; one that I reap returns on daily.

So, are you playing karate? Is it just another leisure activity to pass the time? Or… are you training karate? Are you sacrificing your time and investing in your future?

Only you can answer this.

Training with Injuries

For most of us who train hard in karate, it is inevitable that we will endure some degree of pain and varying degrees of injury at times during our training. The most common are contact related minor injuries such as bruises, sprains, muscle strains, and the occasional broken finger or toe. As we train, we accept these injuries as part of the learning and growth process of the physical side of our martial arts journey. Oftentimes we adapt and continue to train with our injuries. This is both acceptable and encouraged to a point, because it strengthens our spirit and allows us to build the instinct to be flexible and adapt.

> Constant improvement in my skill, character, and health are developed through consistent training, which requires sacrificing my time, comfort, and sometimes money.

Where do we draw the line? Where does common sense overrule the stubborn desire to continue training when we should stop or limit certain facets of training to let our body heal?

The answer lies within us. If we listen to our body, we will know the difference between discomfort and real pain. When we listen to our body, we should also take the next step, and have a physician examine us and then listen to the doctor's advice.

More severe injuries, such as to the back and neck, concussions, fractures, torn muscles, joints injuries of the knees and elbows, may require immediate medical attention. We must swallow our pride and admit that—yes, it's true—we are mortal humans, and none of us are invincible.

A wonderful part of training in traditional karate is that many practitioners enjoy training well into their old age. It is very common to see teachers in Okinawa still training in their 70s and 80s. We can enjoy the health benefits of training, but we have to listen to our bodies when they tells us to slow down and recover.

Forging the Blade

Traditional martial artists train hard. Sweat, blood, tears, bruises, and exhaustion are common—and even expected—at certain points in our training. We spend countless hours practicing basics and kata in the pursuit of perfecting our skill. We constantly put stress on our bodies through strength, endurance, and iron body training. We condition our bodies from our toes to our fingertips and everything in between. Our bodies endure more pain in one training session than the common man can endure.

At least some of us do. Why is this type of *tanren* (severe training) necessary? Is it even necessary? Can we just take it down a few notches and practice kata, kick the heavy bag, and punch the makiwara a couple of times per week? Of course we can. The majority of martial artists train this way, and that's ok for them. The serious martial artists, however, will always push harder, train longer, endure more discomfort, pain, and punishment than their hobbyist peers.

In 1908, Shuri-Te legend Itosu Yasutsune (Anko) wrote:

> "The purpose of karate is to make the muscles and bones hard as rock and to use the hands and legs as spears…"

If our bodies are to be used as weapons, we have a duty to make these weapons as effective as we possibly can. The hottest forge crafts the hardest steel. My challenge to you is to challenge yourself. Hands that rip bamboo, arms and legs that cut through lumber and baseball bats, palms that crush coconuts: these are all impressive feats, but more importantly, these are all perfect examples of someone pushing their limits and forging their weapons to be hard, sharp, and battle ready.

> If we listen to our body, we will know the difference between discomfort and real pain.

These may seem like extreme practices, and other practitioners may even question the validity and effectiveness of this type of training in relation to self-protection/fighting skills. While it is true that tanren alone will not improve our skills, the discipline required to endure this type of training certainly prepares our mind to calmly handle any challenge that we may face, both inside and outside the dojo walls.

A Full Cup of Tea

The longer we train, the more we learn. Over time, we each gain a higher level of skill. Some will go even further and attain mastery of an entire system, sometimes several systems. So, when do you determine that you have all you need? When do you decide that you can't possibly learn any more, or that no one can possibly teach you anything new? The obvious answer is: never. However, it's surprising how common this mentality is within the martial arts community. I've met martial artists that sincerely believe they have such infallible skill, and they can't possibly be taught anything by anyone. This isn't limited to the senior or higher-ranking master-level teachers; I've met and spoken to quite a few intermediate and mid-level practitioners that share this same thought process. Some feel that their teacher or their style offers everything they will ever need, so they don't entertain the idea of being capable of learning from anyone outside of their circle. If you and I ever get to that point, we are finished learning. When our cup is full, it isn't possible to grow anymore. It isn't possible to acquire new skills, or even learn a different method or approach to a skill that we already possess. For martial arts and martial artists to flourish, it is imperative that we always leave a little room in our cup.

In the next chapter, I'll share various topics of my views on training, philosophy, miscellaneous thoughts, opinions, and analogies that don't quite fit into one specific category. Some are personal to me, while others are general principles yet these are personal reflections of what I've learned over the past 30 years.

CHAPTER 5

Rambling

Ronin

In feudal Japan, a masterless samurai was known as *ronin*; a wandering warrior. For any number of reasons—including expulsion, voluntary resignation, or the death of his master—the warrior's ties were cut with his master and he had no home, no income, no affiliation, and thus no one to serve. Often the ronin would wander from village to village, seeking work and affiliation with a new warrior clan. The term *ronin* literally means "wave man." That, however, is an idiomatic expression that means "wandering man," or someone who is without a home. The term originally referred to a serf who had fled or deserted his master's land. It then came to be used for a samurai who had no master. (Hence the term "wave man," meaning one who is socially adrift.) According to the *Bushido Shoshinshu* (the "Code of the Samurai"), a samurai was expected to commit *seppuku* (ritual suicide) upon the loss of his master. One who chose not to honor the code was "on his own" and was meant to suffer great shame. The negative portrayal of ronin status was primarily a discrimination imposed by other samurai and by the feudal lords.

In martial arts there are those that choose to be ronin, or martial artists without a master. They wander from place to place, spending very little time with each master, and usually only stay as long as something benefits them (i.e., rank, recognition, or affiliation). The negative stigma of the ronin of feudal Japan lives on with the modern-day ronin-like martial artists—or wandering warriors. In stark contrast to the ronin of feudal Japan, the ronin martial artist's general traits include questionable loyalty, arrogance, and no concept of *giri* (obligation).

> ...the close-knit relationship between teacher and student, along with the concept of loyalty and obligation, has faded immensely.

While it is quite common, and sometimes even unavoidable, to separate from a teacher or an organization, the martial artist would do well to seek out a new teacher as soon as possible, and, above all, choose only one primary Instructor. With the variety of different martial arts currently available to the public, the average student's approach to training has unfortunately shifted from the old way of being a loyal disciple, to the new way of being a consumer (i.e., paying customer) of martial arts schools. With this change in perspective, it is apparent that the close-knit relationship between teacher and student, along with the concept of loyalty and obligation, has faded immensely.

The old adage, "No man can serve two masters," is still very accurate. In our discussion, we interpret this to mean masters of the same art. Training in different arts is quite beneficial and can be an extraordinarily effective means of raising the skill level of the practitioner. While cross-training in separate arts is beneficial, the martial artist should remain loyal to one primary instructor and *ryu-ha* (style) while keeping in mind that all other martial arts are supplementary and meant to enhance and improve the primary martial art.

The Bridge

As I finished a particularly grueling training session, I was lying on the dojo floor in a pool of sweat trying to catch my breath and cool off. My body was exhausted, but my mind wouldn't shut down as thoughts began to swirl in my head; not unorganized thoughts, mind you, but thoughts of years past and how I'd changed.

I recalled my very first time stepping into the third floor judo dojo of the Columbus YMCA three decades ago. I remember being both nervous and excited, and for some reason—even now—I can remember the smell of sweat and determination that permeated my nose in that stairwell, even before I

opened the door. I remember struggling to tie my first white belt and thinking how gigantic and vicious all of the men were as they threw each other on the mats.

And I trained, refocused, and trained more. As I finished and sat down to cool off, my thoughts drifted again to times past. I remembered meeting my karate sensei for the first time in Okinawa at my friend's wedding. Wade married a beautiful Okinawan lady, and wow, what a wedding they had! To me, it was very elaborate, perhaps even exquisite, as it was the first traditional Okinawan wedding I had ever attended. Sensei and his students demonstrated karate and, although there were other beautiful Okinawan cultural demonstrations, and plenty of delicious food and drink, the karate demo stuck with me.

Immersed in memories of years past, I could see the vivid details replaying in my mind as if they happened yesterday. I remember those Saturday afternoons spent cleaning in and around the dojo and the priceless conversations with Sensei afterwards, sitting on the Sunabe seawall while the waves crashed behind us. I remember struggling so much with every new kata, and with sidekicks because of my lack of natural flexibility. I remember the absolute joy of being appointed to represent our dojo as a coach at the *Okinawa Times* Children's Karate Taikai in 1995, and I remember the sheer terror that I felt when I stepped into the Okinawa Convention Center for the Taikai, and feeling ridiculously unqualified in the presence of so many experienced teachers and practitioners. I remember that same joy and terror rolled into one emotion when my teacher appointed me as his US representative 10 years ago.

So many memories come flooding back when I train, and during the holidays I seem to grow increasingly nostalgic. You see, to me karate isn't just something that I do. Karate—and the culture and traditions that go along with it—is very much a part of me and my daily life. Lessons learned in the dojo can easily be transmitted and practiced in everyday life as well. For most of my life, I have trained and practiced. It's like breathing, I can't imagine functioning without it.

And yet, karate is a bridge. It is a bridge to the past. It's our connection to those that came before us who are now masters—yet they started as a beginner on the very same path that we now travel. It is a bridge to the future as well: those (teachers) that come after us will follow our lead, just as we followed our teachers. As we learn and grow along this journey, let us not ever forget the path that brought us where we are now, and let us always remember that the bridge to the future is just as important as the bridge to the past.

Thoughts on Tradition (Part 1)

Tradition is generally described as an action or belief that is practiced in the present with roots in the past. In karate, our traditional beliefs have been passed through many generations of teachers, and are valued highly because of the ties to our past… a way to connect with our karate forefathers and ancestors.

Many of these traditions are based on an old code of ethics that is deeply rooted in hierarchy and respect. Those of us that consider ourselves traditionalists still practice the old methods; we do so to codify order within the dojo and/or organization.

Many rituals that are observed will seem useless or excessive to the non-traditionalist or inexperienced. The fact is that some rituals serve the very specific purpose of keeping us in touch with humility. There is no place for the arrogant and the braggart in the traditional dojo, and mediocrity is never rewarded.

In our dojo, we all wear the white *keikogi* (training uniform). Although our certified instructors are permitted to wear a black keikogi, they rarely do so. White represents purity and equality in the Japanese tradition. We are reminded when we wear the white keikogi that we are all equal in the sense that we have all started from the beginning, and we are always students on an endless quest for more knowledge, regardless of our experience, rank, or position within the dojo.

Titles and Rank — Although we wear the same uniform to represent equality while helping us to remember our roots and remain humble as we progress, everyone has a very specific place within the dojo. Social standing and age mean nothing within the traditional dojo. No special privileges are given to the wealthy, the famous, or the athletic. All students must work hard to earn their place within the hierarchy of the dojo.

> For most of my life, I have trained and practiced. It's like breathing; I can't imagine functioning without it.

Titles abound for everyone in the dojo. We all have senpai (seniors), as well as kohai (juniors). We have the *dai-senpai*, who usually is the most senior student in the dojo and often the right hand man or woman to the Sensei. It is a bit overwhelming for the new student to remember all the titles; however, they catch on within a week or so.

Sensei or Master — Takamiyagi Hiroshi, my teacher in Okinawa, has been awarded several teaching licenses. *Shihan, kyoshi, and hanshi* are officially recognized master-level licensed teaching titles within Okinawan karate. However, Takamiyagi insists on his students simply calling him Sensei; he will answer to nothing else.

This is humility. A man with so much experience and skill, and yet wishes to be addressed as simply "teacher."

Most Okinawan teachers that I know are the same: highly skilled, very deadly, yet kind and humble.

New Traditions — All traditions have a beginning. Our white keikogi was developed by Jigoro Kano (the founder of Judo) for his students, and was soon adapted for use by the Okinawan karate teachers. Prior to the introduction of the keikogi, there was no uniform for karate students; they often practiced in trousers and t-shirts, or in their underwear. This new tradition of wearing a keikogi served a very functional and utilitarian purpose and was therefore widely accepted and integrated.

Training tools introduced more than a century ago are still in use in the traditional dojo today: the makiwara, *chikara-ishi* (stone weights), and *sashi* (stone padlock), to name a few. These tools are still widely used because they are still functional. They still work. A newer addition to traditional equipment is the heavy bag, which serves a different purpose than the makiwara, and is utilitarian. You will hardly find a traditional karate dojo without a couple of heavy bags hanging from the ceiling.

When is it acceptable to introduce a new tradition into the dojo? Only when it improves the training, development, and skill of the students; but never merely for profit or recognition.

Thoughts on Tradition (Part 2)

Abandoning Tradition — Why do self-proclaimed traditionalists abandon tradition? What plants the seed of thought that tradition is no longer necessary or useful? There are many causes, and I'd like to address a few of them here.

Those who abandon the traditional customs and etiquette of the dojo often claim that it is no longer useful in modern times, for example, to sit in *seiza* (meditation posture) or to bow to the *showmen* (shrine). They will state that calling their teacher "sensei" is antiquated and uncomfortable, and feel it more relaxed just to call each other by first names. When is it acceptable to abandon respect? Of course the answer is "never"!

> Commercialism lies within reach on this one. Many teachers have quite literally left the path of tradition in pursuit of a fatter bank account.

Itosu Anko Sensei wrote the maxim: *"karate begins and ends with respect."* That is to say, respect is constant. We are always a karate student in and out of the dojo; it envelopes our way of life. Therefore, respect never ends, because our karate never ends.

Methods — Some will abandon traditional training methods and remove the study of *bunkai* (analysis) and *oyo* (direct application) from the practice of kata (forms). These teachers simply use kata as another requirement to advance the student's rank, and then move on to the next. These same teachers (and students) will eventually lose interest in kata training, as they will view it as a complete waste of time. In such a case they will be correct, for kata practiced without analysis and direct application is nothing more than dancing.

Why does this happen? Simply put: impatience. Both the teacher and the student lack the patience required for the proper study and practice of kata. It is far easier and faster to "walk-through" a kata and to break a few boards at testing, than it is to teach the intricate details of the "why" we do "what" we do when practicing kata. Details take far too long for the impatient.

It is simply more timely and efficient to teach each and every student to fit the mold, than it is to patiently teach proper body alignment, mechanics, physiology, breathing, and power generation.

Greed — The largest contributor to abandoning tradition in karate is greed. Commercialism lies within reach on this one. Many teachers have quite literally left the path of tradition in pursuit of a fatter bank account.

I want to be very clear on one detail: just because a teacher is successful, he or she should not automatically be branded negatively or classified into the same group as the dreaded "McDojo."

My aim is not to offend those that make their living teaching martial arts. Rather, my aim is to draw attention to the fact that many are teaching modified and ineffective versions of martial arts for no other reason than financial gain: greed.

I know why I began teaching karate nearly 20 years ago. I remember very vividly the reasons why I wanted to share the art that was taught to me by my own teachers. I modeled myself, my teaching methods, and my dojo after my teachers.

The purpose for me is to help guide and develop my students on the path of self-discovery that only traditional training can offer—the joy, disappointment, laughter, tears, sweat, blood, bruises, and exhilaration that come from pushing yourself and training harder. The improved character and integrity that is developed in the traditional dojo is unmatched. This is why I teach, not for money, or recognition. If money and recognition come, great! If not, great! I have, and will always remain, a traditionalist.

With thousands of karate dojo all over the globe, there are just as many different ways to practice as there are karate styles to choose from. Some have embraced a modern, sports-oriented, or less difficult approach to old karate training methods. Far fewer have kept and embrace the old ways to forge themselves and their students.

Old School

I hear it often, and some of you reading this may hear it too: "You guys are old school." Most say it approvingly—almost as a congratulatory statement. Some say it in an accusatory tone. Others say it out of surprise. To me, it's a compliment, a badge of honor, an indisputable fact.

What is "old school training?"

My definition is simply training in the same manner and using the same methods that were standard practice in the Okinawan dojo decades ago. It doesn't mean resisting change or keeping a closed mind; it simply means embracing the traditional, functional methods. I'll provide a list of examples that I like, and equate with old-school training:

Chibana Choshin 1885-1969. Founder of Shorin-Ryu

I like to wear a white karate-gi with only one patch. I have different gi/*hakama* for iaido, judo, and organizational events. In Japan, there is a term, *shibumi*, which means simple elegance. I like that principle in everything. No superfluous patches, stripes, or anything else to distract from training, or draw attention to the wearer.

I like a wood floor. We have mats on our main dojo training area with 100 yr. old hardwood underneath, but I prefer training — especially kata — on a wood floor.

I like training barefoot, indoors or outdoors. In karate, so many details are in the toes- gripping, turning, balance, and power transfer that are lost when shoes are worn.

> The improved character and integrity that is developed in the traditional dojo is unmatched. This is why I teach, not for money, or recognition.

I like to train in a hot dojo in the summer and a cold dojo in the winter; extremes help forge discipline of the mind. A disciplined mind creates a disciplines karateka.

I like to sweat... a lot. Even in the winter, I like to sweat. If I haven't soaked my gi and undergarments with sweat during training, I feel as if I haven't worked hard enough.

I like training outdoors. I train in the grass, on my patio, or on the roof of my dojo. Training outdoors, being in touch with nature, brings me closer to the source.

I like the old, tried and proven methods and hojo undo equipment. Our dojo has kicking shields, hand targets, heavy bags, benches, barbells and dumbbells. We also have makiwara, chi-ishi, ironman training dummy, and at home I have *ishi-bako, nigiri ga-me* (gripping jars), ishi-sashi (stone locks similar to kettlebells) and various other iron palm and iron finger training equipment. I prefer the older tools to the newer ones.

I like contact; lots of contact, solo (with training tools), or with a partner, soft and hard. Contact is the key to learning about your body mechanics, pain threshold, and pushing your limits.

I like a simple, functional dojo. We have what we need to train, learn, and grow. The most luxurious item in our dojo is the drink cooler; it keeps the water and Gatorade chilled and refreshing. No juice bar. No parents' lounge. No flat screen TV on the wall.

> Some will question your methods, some will chastise you, and some will misunderstand and call you closed-minded. Don't let it bother you.

To be clear, I find absolutely nothing wrong with modern equipment, or wearing a different uniform (if required by your teacher or organization). Air conditioning and heat are great amenities, and perhaps even necessary for any public dojo that wants to attract parents and their children. Varying levels of contact and foam armor (sparring gear) are the norm for many dojos in modern times. This is due in part to insurance regulations; but honestly, most people just don't like getting hit. Flat screen TVs, Wi-Fi, and lounges are great luxuries, and for my friends that have large, professional karate dojo's I would even venture to agree that these amenities may be a necessary business expense.

Does this mean you have to stand and choose between old-school and modern? No. Everyone can embrace some of the old-school ways. Even if your dojo has modern and luxurious amenities, your training methods can still be "old school." If you are one of those old school karateka, understand that you are in the ever-increasing minority; some will question your methods, some will chastise you, some will misunderstand and call you closed-minded. Don't let it bother you. Take that compliment, wear that badge of honor, and pass it on to the next generation.

This was a brief look into my personal beliefs of martial arts training, philosophy, and expectations based on both experiences and lessons taught by my teachers. The following chapter is directed toward all students, including those of us who are now teachers, for no matter how much experience and skill we gain, we should always remain a humble student.

CHAPTER 6

Students

Coming Home

In Okinawa there is a saying: *"Ichariba chodee."* When we meet, we are brothers. There are several variations of this interpretation, but this is the basic one. Okinawan people (Uchinanchu) are very welcoming, friendly, and trusting in general. When you meet for the first time, and you share a common bond—karate, culture, or food—you will often have a friend for life. The Okinawan karate dojo is an extension of this exquisite culture, and much to the surprise of many *gaijin* (foreigners) the Okinawan way of life is laid back and relaxed both in and out of the dojo. Yes, you are expected to work hard, push yourself, exceed your limits, but you will not have a teacher pushing and prodding you like a drill instructor.

Your *shinshii* (teacher) will take on the role of father-figure to all of his students. He will teach, lead, and guide you along the path to karate mastery,

and in turn you will come to respect him as more than a teacher. The bond of respect is nurtured through hard training, dedication to your art, and loyalty to your teacher and dojo.

Life happens and people move on, move away, become ill, injured, or sometimes change priorities. For many different reasons, the student and teacher become separated. This happened to me when I left Okinawa to return to my hometown in Georgia; yet, although I was physically separated from my teacher, I always remained dedicated and loyal to him and all that he taught me. Takamiyagi Sensei has rewarded my loyalty and dedication in more ways than I ever imagined, and although we don't see one another for long periods of time, every single homecoming is a sweet reunion. It's as if we were never apart, and after a celebration party or two, it's always back to training, learning, and reinforcing exactly why I remain loyal to this man, as I am taught even more intricate details of our art, while being reminded just how little I have learned.

As a teacher, I too have had students move on, move away, and stop training for a variety of reasons over the past 15 years that I've taught at the Columbus Dojo. Sometimes they return, and when they do, it's a sweet homecoming. The bond that was initially formed is strengthened, loyalty is renewed, and dedication is shown once again.

This week, I'm looking forward to a couple of students coming home; both have been away for over a year, but have kept in contact and have remained loyal to the dojo. As a teacher, the warm feeling of a student coming home to the dojo can be compared to a father welcoming his son home after a long absence. Friends, if you have been away from your dojo and your teacher for a while, be sure to contact them to touch base and maybe let them know that you appreciate them, and are grateful for what they've taught you.

I make sure to call my Sensei at least once or twice a month just to chat and say thank you. Whether he admits it or not, I know he likes to hear the words, "*Takamiyagi Shinshii-Zenbu Oshieta no koto nifuedebiiru* (Takamiyagi Sensei, thank you for all that you've taught me)."

Giri — The True Student/Teacher Connection

After training this afternoon, I began to reminisce of the time I had with my teacher in Okinawa, and the amount of time and sweat it took before he recognized that my loyalty was genuine. My loyalty was measured not in *yen* (money) or gifts to Sensei, but in being at the dojo training every single time the door was unlocked. I spent literally thousands of hours training under the watchful eye of Takamiyagi Sensei in the years that I lived in Okinawa. I spent hundreds of hours maintaining and cleaning the dojo inside and out, and on Saturday mornings, my private giri was to clean the weeds and trash from the outside of the dojo.

After a few months, Sensei drove by the dojo one Saturday morning and caught me; he told me that he suspected one of his students had been secretly cleaning the dojo grounds and wanted to see who it was.

He never opened the dojo that day. Instead he said, "Take a break, let's walk." We walked the short block from the dojo to the Sunabe seawall. Sensei purchased two *oolong-cha* (tea) from a nearby vending machine, and we sat on the seawall watching the waves crash while we talked for an hour or so. During the course of conversation, he asked when I had started cleaning the dojo grounds, and why I was doing it. His expression became serious; not quite angry, but very stern. Honestly, I was worried that he thought I was trying to "brown-nose" and was sure that I was about to get scolded. I told Sensei that it had been a few weeks since I started cleaning, and I did it because it needed to be done, and because I take pride in my dojo. (The truth is, weeks ago after class, I was walking to my car

Takamiyagi Hiroshi and the author at Takamiyagi Sensei's home in Chatan-Cho, Okinawa. 2003

> When a student sacrifices time, money, or effort for his teacher, it should always be recognized and appreciated.

and dropped my keys—because the grass was so tall and thick, it took me a few minutes to find them.) I had really only planned to clean outside the dojo that one time, but I felt obligated to come back again, and again. It felt great to have a responsibility of my own at the dojo. (Of course, I left that part out).

Sensei smiled and said, *"Joto* (very good*),"* then changed the subject.

Although we had 5-10 minute conversations in the past, it was always in the dojo and with a group of other students; this was the longest that Sensei had ever spoken to me, and the first time for a one-on-one conversation. After talking for a while, he said, "Let's go eat," so we walked a few blocks to *Hamaya Soba* for what would become a Saturday tradition for the next couple of years. After we ate, I thanked Sensei for lunch, and we parted ways.

I would come to the dojo on Saturday mornings to clean, and then Sensei would show up right around lunch time. We walked and talked about karate, philosophy, life and love; I listened to advice and stories of the old masters, I learned and our bond grew closer. Sensei later invited me to his home for lunch and dinner and I was accepted and welcomed warmly by his family. Strangely, the term giri never came up during any conversation. I had no idea of the terminology defining obligation, duty, and loyalty, but I certainly understood the concept. I felt obligated then, as I do now, to do whatever I could to help Sensei, to help the dojo, and to find small ways to let him know that I was truly grateful for all that he shared with me.

Giri Explained

I believe that even without being tutored on the details of giri, every serious karateka of good character is drawn to the practice like a moth to a flame. And although the concept of giri can be taught and lectured on an intellectual level, the practitioner has to feel the desire within himself for it to be genuinely appreciated. Quite simply, as a student I carry a debt of obligation to my teacher for all that he has done. In turn, I endeavor to repay that debt by showing my loyalty through doing whatever I can to help my teacher, and the dojo.

The side of giri that most forget about is that it is always reciprocal. When the student attempts to repay a debt of obligation to the teacher through different methods of personal sacrifice, then that teacher will often feel obligated to share even more with the dedicated student as a reward for loyalty. And the cycle continues. When a student sacrifices time, money, or effort for the teacher, it should always be recognized and appreciated. Sometimes, it's something as simple as Sensei acknowledging you and picking up the lunch tab on Saturday.

In the years that I lived and trained in Okinawa, the time spent in the dojo learning and practicing will always be priceless, but the private time—those hundreds of hours that I had with my Sensei—I'll cherish forever.

An Open Letter to Students

This is an open letter to students: new students, experienced students, young students and old students, my students, and your students—if you have them. This letter defines, in simplest terms, the formula for your success in martial arts. Conversely, this letter also highlights some common issues that prevent martial arts success, and guides you through that challenge.

In finance, ROI is the acronym for and is used to measure your Return on Investment; or more simply put, the benefits expected from your sacrifice, time, money, and effort.

A performance measure can be used to evaluate the efficiency of an investment or to compare the efficiency of a number of different investments. To calculate ROI, the benefit (return) of an investment is divided by the cost of the investment; the result is expressed as a percentage or a ratio. The return on investment formula is:

$$ROI = \frac{(\text{Gain from Investment} - \text{Cost of Investment})}{\text{Cost of Investment}}$$

In the above formula "gains from investment," refers to the proceeds obtained from selling the investment of interest. Return on investment is a very popular metric because of its versatility and simplicity. That is, if an investment does not have a positive ROI, or if there are other opportunities with a higher ROI, then the investment should be not be undertaken. What does this have to do with martial arts? Everything! Read on.

Training — Every single time that we step into the dojo to train, we are preparing to make an investment in our future self. On the most basic level, this investment consists of hard work, sweat, and the willingness to follow directions, on the most basic level. Those that are willing to sacrifice their time, effort, ego, and comfort will see almost immediate benefits, and these benefits are continuous and long term — as long as the investment continues. Those that train daily will most certainly benefit from their investment much quicker than those that train sporadically. (See the formula above.)

Conversely, those that train once or twice per week, and only show up at the dojo sporadically, will be waiting much longer to benefit from their investment. Yet, it's usually the ones that train inconsistently that are the most easily discouraged and even impatient. They don't understand why their dojo classmate has been taught more, and sometimes even promoted above themselves when they started training at the same time. The formula is simple. The ROI is based on commitment, dedication and loyalty of the karate student. Invest more time, reap more benefits. It really is that simple!

Loyalty —The first investment in yourself is training consistently. The second investment is loyalty - to yourself, your teacher, your dojo. How dedicated are you to your dojo and your particular style of martial arts? If you're training hard, I know that you're committed to yourself, but are you committed to your teacher and giving back to the dojo? Are you committed to being an ambassador of the dojo and your particular martial arts system? Or are you in it just for yourself? If you truly want to grow and be a leader, you must give back (time, not money).

You can't buy loyalty or special favors in lieu of time invested (at least not in a reputable dojo).

When it's time to train, be there. On time. When the dojo sponsors or hosts in-house training events, or travels to support others—be there. When a junior student is struggling, don't wait for them to ask for help—be there. Here's the little-known secret practiced by the Okinawan masters; are you ready for it? Loyalty is rewarded. Let me say it again, *loyalty is rewarded*. Why? Loyalty is synonymous with trust and respect. When you prove your loyalty, you earn the trust and respect from your teacher. That's the old way, and it works great.

Talk is Cheap

If you say you're going to do something, do it. Period. Talk is cheap, and excuses are worthless. Your reputation is on the line every time you make a commitment, every time you make a promise, and every single time you say, "I'll be there."

Students of all ages and experience levels, from beginner to instructor, take a few minutes to evaluate yourself, and your commitment to investing in your future self. Are you doing all that you can for yourself, and for your dojo, your teacher, and your future? If so, that's fantastic; keep up the good work! If not, why? Do you feel that you should be at a higher skill level than you are currently? Yes? Then do something about it! Put your priorities in order and start investing. Commit. Be unwavering. Do not allow excuses to interfere with your success!

There are no free rides in martial arts. If you want skill, you have to earn it. If you want respect, you have to earn it. If you want to rise through the ranks, you have to earn the respect of your teacher through commitment, dedication, and loyalty.

Return on investment: no reward for mediocrity. The leaders of tomorrow are forged from the sacrifice of sweat and hard work of today.

Next Time

I love to train and learn new things, and I really love to teach—especially when I'm able to witness a student's mental awakening when they finally "get it." It's a fantastic and humbling feeling to influence a person's success in even the smallest way; the feeling is almost indescribable!

> **Loyalty is synonymous with trust and respect. When you prove your loyalty, you earn the trust and respect of your teacher.**

To us, karate is a *way of life*, and a passion that only grows stronger as we continue to practice and learn. We teachers and senior students have committed ourselves to a life of constant learning and improvement in the effort to guide our students down the martial path, and to achieve balance for ourselves.

> There are no free rides in martial arts. If you want skill, you have to earn it. If you want respect, you have to earn it.

As a teacher, I have grown in skill and patience when dealing with new students, and the seemingly lazier generation that is springing up. Laziness can be cured by proper guidance, character development, focus, and goal-setting, so it isn't an unsolvable issue.

Commitment—that's altogether different. Every year at this time, I receive texts and emails (but oddly, no phone calls) from adults informing me that they won't be able to attend this year due to (insert excuse here) but, *"I'll definitely be there next time."* These are the ones that commit (verbally) and then wait until a day or two before the event to cancel. Is this a new trend? Absolutely not. In the 15 years that I've taught, organized and hosted events, I've had the last-minute "maybe next time" cancellations from strangers, guest instructors, and students — every single year.

For those readers that have also hosted or promoted events, you're probably shaking your head right now because you've experienced the same "next-timers." Granted, there are always valid reasons or excuses for absences and non-attendance. Sometimes life situations and unavoidable emergencies arise; these cases are always understandable and excusable.

This isn't a gripe session or a rant, nor is it a call to action. This is simply recognition of people and their behavior based on their level of commitment. This is a gentle nudge to check your level of commitment and integrity.

Enlightenment happens now; nothing happens "next time."

Dojo Shomen: Okinawa Goshukan-Ryu USA Honbu Dojo

The Timeless Dojo

Weeks, months, or years—it doesn't matter to the dojo how long you've been away. Priorities change. Responsibilities change. Schedules change. People change. Yet, the dojo is waiting for your return. It is unassuming, with no hidden agenda, no pride, no anger, no criticism, no disappointment.

The hardwood and the mats are waiting for your feet to grab and move, waiting for your sweat to drip, waiting for your body to land in its embrace. The makiwara, the chi-ishi, the weapons, the heavy bags, shields, pads, and weights—they all wait patiently for your return. They are all essential tools in the dojo, tools to build a better you. But without you, they are useless ornaments.

These tools and the dojo do not judge; they don't choose favorites. Everyone is equal. Everyone has the opportunity to be better, faster, and stronger. The dojo will help you, whenever you're ready.

Teachers will come and go. Some are skilled. Some are not. Some teachers will open your eyes and inspire you. Some will change your life forever. Even the teacher knows the secret to success: go to the dojo, just one more time.

Friends, students, and readers: my life has changed direction significantly over the past few years. Free time is not a luxury for me any longer as I work toward new goals. Burnout is always lurking just around the corner. What keeps me going on the hardest of days is this: the dojo is waiting for me; I have to go… I *have* to go. Just for today. When I walk up the stairs, and into that timeless dojo, I have peace knowing that I will leave a better person than when I walked in. I know that the dojo has been patiently waiting for me, and I know… I'm home.

Without teachers, there would be no students; and without students to learn, we would have no need for teachers. We need each other, and should always keep in mind that there are many lessons learned as a student that teachers should absolutely remember. The following chapter addresses teachers from both a student and a peer viewpoint.

CHAPTER 7

Teachers

Sensei's Hat

In this section I'd like to cover a topic that martial arts teachers know all too well. Yet, it may shed some light on the subject matter for the newer students, the uninitiated, or the unobservant. It will be short, concise, and casual, in that it is straight talk from me about my experiences to you, the reader.

As long as teachers have been teaching, they have been brilliant multi-taskers, whether they wanted to be or not. In any single day, we can wear a half dozen or more "hats." I few of the hats that I have been and continue to wear, include: janitor, painter, handyman, plumber, enrollment specialist, medic, mediator, parent, mentor, bookkeeper, accountant, fundraiser, inventory control specialist, event organizer and host, life coach, teacher, student, superhero, supervillain.

Of course there are probably another dozen or two that I've missed, but you get the point. As you read the list, you were likely nodding your head in agreement, as you realized all of the different "hats" that your sensei wears on a daily basis. Then there are the last two, which probably had you scratching your head.

Superhero and supervillain? Let me explain. You see, I've had two teachers in my first thirty years of training. My judo teacher, Schmitt Sensei, and my karate teacher, Takamiyagi Sensei. Both men helped inspire, mold, and shape me in their own way. Both were capable of feats that (at the time) I didn't quite understand. To me, they were superhuman. Now as a more experienced martial artist, I have begun to understand how and why my teachers were able to do what they did, and I have even replicated some of it in my own training.

To the new student, we are superheroes: we do things that they can't yet fathom, only due to their inexperience, and they will come to understand, just as I did, with time and experience.

To some, we are the supervillain: the nuance has worn off, and students quickly understand that they have to actually work very hard to see results and improvements. Some students will vilify their sensei for making it look so easy while relentlessly requiring more sweat, effort, and pain from the student.

Next time your sensei seems a little absent-minded or forgets that he's already covered the material that you are being taught for the first time, try to show a little compassion and understanding. Although sensei is wearing the teacher hat right now, there may be a dozen other hats that were worn before class that day.

Gratitude

> *"Gratitude bestows reverence, allowing us to encounter everyday epiphanies, those transcendent moments of awe that change forever how we experience life and the world."* —John Milton

Schmitt Sensei — In 1984, as a sophomore in high school, I climbed the steps to the third floor of the YMCA for the first time with my father. With every step, the thumps became louder, and as I stepped into the judo room I was in awe of the dozen men in sweaty white keikogi as they threw each other to the ground and hopped back up, unfazed. This was the beginning of my martial arts journey. I am forever indebted to my father for allowing me to train, and for my first sensei, Alfred Schmitt, for teaching me the value and true meaning of perseverance.

Military — Fast forward a few years: after high school I worked a few jobs, became bored with life, and on a whim visited my local Air Force recruiter. A few months later, I began basic training at Lackland Air Force Base in Texas and began my new military career. When I was stationed in Korea, I visited a couple of Tang Soo Do *dojang* (schools) but found another *judoka* working out on the Osan Air Base at the gym; he was more experienced than me and became my training partner for the remainder of my tour. Following my tour in Korea, I was stationed in Kadena Air Base in Okinawa. Although I was intent on continuing my journey in judo, I met another young martial artist in my barracks, we became friends, and this friendship changed the direction of my martial arts journey. Wade Chroninger introduced me to Takamiyagi

Hiroshi Sensei, his karate teacher, and the founder of Goshukan-ryu. I was accepted as a student of Takamiyagi Sensei and began training at the Hamagawa Dojo; Wade and I worked together, and he helped me immensely in my first year of training. He and I would train from time to time at lunch or on weekends. Although Wade left the Hamagawa Dojo and pursued training in Meibukan Goju-ryu, he was very influential in the direction of my martial arts journey; indeed, if Wade had not introduced me to his teacher, I would not be writing this—perhaps I would not even be training.

I am grateful to the USAF for the opportunity to travel to Okinawa, and I am grateful to my good friend of twenty-plus years, Wade Chroninger, for introducing me to Takamiyagi Sensei over two decades ago.

Takamiyagi Sensei — I finished my tour with the USAF and made the transition to civilian life. Takamiyagi Sensei helped me find an apartment close to the dojo and was instrumental in my ability to accomplish everyday tasks such as setting up utilities and banking. He became like a second father to me when I was in Okinawa and taught me life lessons in and out of the dojo. Takamiyagi Sensei encouraged me to continually challenge myself, push hard, and enjoy training. He taught me the meaning of giri (the concept of obligation and duty in Japanese culture and martial arts). Although I had great instruction when training at the dojo, some of my fondest memories are weekend afternoons: on Saturday or Sunday I would often go to the dojo early to clean and cut weeds around the dojo property, not because I was asked, but because I felt a sense of duty to take care of the dojo. Takamiyagi Sensei would come to the dojo around noon, and we walked a few blocks to have lunch at Hamaya Soba, then on to the seawall in Sunabe. These few hours were spent discussing the finer details of Okinawan Karate, history, philosophy and of course, stories. I cherish those moments that my Sensei shared so much of his personal time and experiences with me. After being promoted to black belt, Takamiyagi Sensei tasked me with teaching the beginner children in 1995, and that was the beginning of my teaching experience.

America — In September 1996 I returned to America, and continued to train on my own while searching for a new dojo and training partners. I trained police officers and sheriff deputies, but had no dojo to call home. In 1998, I began construction of a small private dojo in my own backyard so that I would always have a place to train, and although I trained constantly, I was frustrated at the lack of feedback and instruction. I spent hundreds of dollars every month on long-distance phone calls to Okinawa, always asking questions and seeking advice from Takamiyagi Sensei.

One particular evening as I was feeling very frustrated, I called Sensei again, and told him that I was considering moving back to Okinawa (I thought he would be thrilled to have his only American student come back). Instead, he asked, "Why?" I explained that I needed him to guide me and teach me more, and that I had no place to train in my city; there were no other Okinawan Karate dojos here. Sensei encouraged me to teach a few family and friends in the dojo that I had just built; I objected on the basis that I was too young and inexperienced. He told me to teach "kihon and two kata" and to return to Okinawa every year for intense private training with him. I objected again, but finally agreed. In March 1999, the Okinawa Goshukan-Ryu Columbus Shibu/Branch Dojo held its first classes with my wife, brother-in-law, and one coworker.

I am eternally grateful for my teacher, Takamiyagi Sensei, for having faith in me when I had none, for seeing the future growth when I saw only frustration, and for trusting me enough to be the very first person in America to teach his style of martial arts.

Finally, I am grateful to my wife, Izumi, for being right beside me on my journey, and sometimes falling behind just far enough to give me a push. I am grateful to my students, without whom there would be no need for a teacher. I am grateful for the scores of friends that I have met and trained with over the years through the practice of martial arts.

After reading this, you may be asking why this was included in the "Teachers" chapter. Very simple: No matter how high we climb, we as teachers should always remember our roots, and always show sincere respect and humble gratitude to those that have been instrumental in our journey.

This brings us to our next chapter: Character. We all have it. Some good, some bad, some flawless, and some questionable. What does this have to with martial arts practice? Can someone with good character learn more quickly? Can someone with bad character be entrusted with advanced concepts and techniques? Read on.

CHAPTER 8

Character

Prejudice in the Dojo

The white *keikogi* was implemented in Okinawa nearly a century ago. This served two purposes: the first was function, the second served as a social equalizer, a prejudice terminator. Every student in the dojo wore a plain white gi in those early years of the newly formalized public karate dojo in Okinawa. The uniformity erased class lines, and even today serves this same purpose.

Today, there are other prejudices in the dojo, and nearly all of them remain hidden except to the trained eye or ear. Let me elaborate. In the karate dojo, we enjoy a relationship that is both familial and militaristic. We do have a set chain of command (sensei, senpai, kohai), while we also are a tight-knit group of brothers and sisters in *budo* (martial arts). With family comes compassion, and with hierarchy comes expectations. This is a delicate balance in the dojo, and one that I feel needs to be addressed for all of us.

Example 1 — A student arrives to class for the first time in two weeks. This student has been attending sporadically over the past few months; it is evident that he hasn't been practicing at home. In fact, it is evident that the student's overall skill has diminished. Other students smile and greet the returning dojo brother and are genuinely happy to see him in class again. One of the seniors, however, makes a snide comment: *"It's about time you came back, and you obviously have some catching up to do."* The senior has judged the returning student without *any* information about his absence. If the senior had taken the time to ask either the returning student or the teacher, he would have learned that the returning student recently changed jobs and was now working rotating shifts, which prevented the student from attending classes on a regular basis. Now, for the first time in weeks, the

> The original purpose of martial arts training is for self-protection and the defense of others. However, there are tremendous additional benefits other than self-protection.

student was so happy to finally be able to train again and was greeted with smiles and open arms, only to be criticized by a senior without even a "hello." Because of this, the returning student now begins to question if he really wants to continue training at this dojo; after all, one of the main tenets of the traditional dojo is mutual respect, and the senior had not shown any at all.

Example 2 — Your dojo brother has been training with you for five years. You have always trained together and learned from one another, one even feeding off the energy of the other. Recently, you notice that your dojo brother has not been moving as fast or kicking as hard as he normally does. Instead of speaking to your brother and asking if you can help, you accuse your dojo brother of slacking. He says nothing, and in a few weeks, he's no longer attending classes. You assume that his laziness has taken precedence over commitment, and don't even bother to contact him.

What really happened? Had you spoken to your dojo brother and asked what was going on, you would've been informed of his recent diagnosis of Type 2 diabetes. The medication and disease have been sapping his energy, and quite honestly, he's been a little depressed as well. The dojo was his single outlet; he looked forward to class every single week, knowing he was in control just for a few hours. Instead of receiving support from his dojo brother and partner, he was scolded for slowing down and accused of being lazy. Now with his faith shaken, he decides to quit.

The previous examples are fictitious accounts; however, this type of incident is more common than most people realize. Arrogance and ignorance are the primary causes of judging others. Humble yourselves and educate yourselves, and most importantly, treat others the way you want to be treated (the Golden Rule).

Students and teachers alike: if you notice a change in your dojo brothers and sisters, your seniors and juniors, your students and teachers—communicate with them. Be polite and genuinely compassionate; do not judge them. There may be much more going on than you see on the surface. Remember that every single student has his own personal reason for training, and it may not be your reason. That's ok, too.

Yes, the original purpose of martial arts training is for self-protection and the defense of others. However, there are tremendous additional benefits other than self-protection. As students mature and gain more experience, their goals may change. A thirty-year-old male in his prime physical condition is going to train differently than a forty-five-year-old female and mother. The important thing is that everyone trains to the best of their own ability. A good instructor understands that karate training is not "cookie-cutter" training. There is no single mold that everyone must be forced to fit; a wise student will accept this and understand this as well.

Friends, teachers, and students: train hard and judge only yourself.

Out of Order

Karate has a multitude of benefits—this fact is uncontested by all who practice. Self-defense and life protection are the primary purposes of karate. In addition, consistent training yields such benefits as:

- Discipline
- Self-control
- Self-confidence
- Improved health
- Improved focus
- Improved self-esteem
- Increased stamina
- Increased speed and strength
- Stress relief

> There is no single mold that everyone must be forced to fit; a wise student will accept this and understand this as well.

The list could go on and on, but you get the idea. These are some of the most common benefits of karate. More importantly, we should always strive to seek perfection of character, to live a life of honor and integrity, to strive for constant improvement of the body, mind, and spirit, and to remain humble in all that is accomplished.

In recent years, I have spoken to several former students that have expressed interest in resuming their training. Regardless of the reason they stopped training, I always ask why they want to return. Too many have told me, "I just need ten minutes on the heavy bag" or "I need to work out some of this stress."

Friends and students, while these are very valid parts of training, they are not the primary reasons. If we are angry, we need to improve our discipline so that we maintain self-control. If we are overstressed, we must remove ourselves from the things or people that cause us stress, and if we can't remove ourselves, we should strive to find balance and improve our focus on what is important in our lives first.

Proper karate training benefits the whole person, inside and out. If we focus only on the physical benefits of training, our karate is out of order.

Moments that Define You

This topic is not bound to the subject of karate; actually, it's a collection of observations that can be understood and applied by everyone.

No matter our station in life, there are moments that define us all. For some, these defining moments are raw, instinctive, or unplanned. For others, the defining moment is the culmination of years of meticulous planning and preparation. As you read the following names, you will recognize most of them for their defining moments: Amelia Earhart, Jonas Salk, Alexander Graham Bell . . . then there's John Wilkes Booth and Theodore (Ted) Kaczynski.

Their defining moments made American history. The first woman to fly solo across the Atlantic Ocean. The inventor of the polio vaccine. The inventor of the telephone. All made their marks on history through their defining moments. John Wilkes Booth and Theodore Kaczynski also left their mark on history: one assassinated Abraham Lincoln, and the other was known as the Unabomber.

> Most of us are merely ordinary humans. Yet we all have the capacity and the capability to become extraordinary!

Ordinary humans accomplish extraordinary things every single day; some become famous, some remain anonymous. Most of us are merely ordinary humans. Yet we all have the capacity and the capability to become extraordinary! Find something that you love—something that you are passionate about—and put your heart and soul into it every single day. When we contribute to the betterment of our fellow man and the improvement of society, we feel better because we have a true purpose in life.

When we realize that our purpose in this life is more about what we can do for others than what we can do for ourselves, we open the doors of opportunity to make a positive difference in so many lives. Every single day that we wake up, we are given the chance to make a moment that defines us. We make the choice to do good, bad, or nothing at all. Choose wisely.

> Every single day that we wake up, we are given the chance to make a moment that defines us. We make the choice to do good, bad, or nothing at all. Choose wisely.

What drives our character also shapes our will. The physical side of karate training has been covered in detail, and while the physical training is most visible, we must remember that nothing is accomplished without the power of our minds.

CHAPTER 9

Shin (The Mind)

The power to succeed, fail, grow, and change is within you. We all have it within us. Extraordinary acts are accomplished every day by ordinary people just like you and me.

What sets apart the ordinary from the extraordinary? Is our DNA code different? Are we genetically determined to be above average? What factors determine who will be the next great inventor, physician, artist, or philosopher? Will we ever see another Nikola Tesla, Jonas Salk, George Washington Carver, or Socrates in our lifetime?

What is it that drives us to succeed? Friends, we may not have the mind of Albert Einstein, the creative genius of Leonardo DaVinci, or the focus and physical prowess of Miyamoto Musashi; however, we have the greatest force in our world that drives us to persevere, failure after failure, until we achieve our goals.

Nothing is greater than the absolute power of the mind. Within our mind lies the power of *in/yo* (yin/yang) or positive and negative. Our minds can allow us to achieve things that are seemingly impossible by driving us to continue, even as our bodies are ready to give up.

Conversely, our minds can deal a crushing blow to our aspirations of success by allowing doubt and fear to set in. Our minds can become a breeding ground for the poison of negativity. Our minds become weak and allow us to create excuses to quit instead creating reasons to persevere, fight harder, and achieve.

How then do we control what direction our mind will lead us? The answer is simple, the act is not. We control what we allow into our minds. Refrain from

> Mushin is a mental and emotional state in which we can see clearly. A mind void of the clutter of our busy lives and void of the distractions around us.

negativity; do not allow it into your ears or your mind, and especially, do not allow negativity to come out of your mouth.

We are mere humans, yet we continually shock and amaze ourselves as a species when we constantly crash through our walls of impossibilities.

Do something great for yourself today: set your goal and achieve it. You can do it, for within you lies the absolute power of your mind.

Beginner's Mind

In karate dojos throughout Okinawa and Japan, the concept of *shoshin* (beginner's mind) is commonly taught to students—especially intermediate and senior students. The concept and practice of beginner's mind is a valuable lesson in humility for all students, regardless of skill level and experience.

The brown-belt student and the black-belt teacher alike can benefit from shoshin. Remember the first day, week, or month of training in a new dojo? Remember the overwhelming excitement, the realization that you know nothing, the thirst for knowledge that could never be quenched?

That is beginner's mind. That is shoshin. A student should always remain excited, thirsty for knowledge, and above all realize that no matter how much skill and experience they acquire, there is always much more to learn—in the mind of the beginner.

Remaining Mind

To be vigilant and always ready is *zanshin*. It's not a place, an event, or attitude—zanshin is a state of mind. It doesn't mean that we should live our lives in a constant state of paranoia; no, quite the opposite is true. We should remain calm, sharp, and ready for anything. Zanshin means not letting your guard down even in social situations or at home where we are most comfortable. Simply put, pay attention to all of your surroundings, all of the time. We should never get so comfortable with people or places that we completely let our guard down.

Empty Mind

Mushin. Mu is void, not in the sense of being empty of all thought, but in the sense of being void of conscious distraction. Mushin embodies the very essence of the warrior. Mushin enables us to overcome fear, doubt, uncertainty, and distraction in order to focus fully on the task at hand. Mushin isn't living in the moment. Mushin is becoming the moment.

Mushin—the empty mind, or clear mind—is a mental and emotional state in which we can see clearly. A mind void of the clutter of our busy lives and void of the distractions around us. Mushin is not empty, as in void of all thought; on the contrary, this state of mind allows us to see clearly everything around us, allowing us to focus one hundred percent of our effort with no distractions.

Think of your mind as a pool of water. When the water is still, it clearly reflects everything around it: the blue sky above, rustling tree branches, swaying grass, and gently falling leaves. Drop the smallest pebble in the water and it ripples—small at first, and increasingly larger until the entire pool of water is rippled. Everything becomes distorted and blends in the reflection of the water. The trees, the sky, the grass, and the leaf; everything from the wide open to the smallest detail has distorted into a rippling mass of confusion and chaos.

We have control of our minds and what goes in and stays in. Let your pond remain clear and still. This is mushin, and it will effectively enhance your personal growth in the dojo and in life.

Kaizen

Before I was able to apply the term to karate study, it was drilled into my coworkers and me by our bosses at CB Koei Company in Okinawa, Japan. The year was 1994, and I had recently separated from active duty and been hired by a local company as an apprentice mason.

The term *kaizen* was heard every morning during our daily meeting, and at least once weekly we were called on to explain and demonstrate our ideas for kaizen. What is it? Kaizen is a process of constant improvement. The kanji means, "to make good." To understand kaizen, we must understand the concept of making good or improving. Although Toyota first streamlined the concept decades ago for use in the manufacturing industry, kaizen is nothing new. Any endeavor can be made more efficient and more effective through the process of constant improvement.

What does this have to do with karate? Every time we practice, we do so with the intent of improving—we have the goal of learning more, practicing harder, and gaining more skill. Yet sometimes we fall short. How can we maximize our efficiency when training? Do we work harder or practice longer? Yes, and no. First, we must analyze how we are training. We must determine if we are using methods that are counterproductive to progress, and if so, we have to make changes. By making small and consistent changes to our training process, we are constantly improving our learning ability.

What are these changes? Those of you with regular teachers should seek the advice on details from your teachers. Something as simple as being well rested before you practice or clearing your mind of distractions before you train will help prepare your mind and body for learning.

Understand that kaizen is the concept of improving an existing process (training method); kaizen is not the concept of replacing or changing an existing process (training method). Every one of us can always find some small way to improve.

> **Something as simple as being well rested before you practice or clearing your mind of distractions before you train will help prepare your mind and body for learning.**

Sometimes the issue is driven by external forces beyond our control; more commonly, the issue is within us, and we have the power to change the process.

Kaizen will always be synonymous with progress and growth. There are proper methods of living and training that lead to progress, and there are issues that impede growth. We'll address both of these in the next chapter.

CHAPTER 10

Growth

Baggage

Part 1. Life — The dojo can be a place of escape for many practitioners. Clark Kent has the fortress of solitude, Bruce Wayne has the bat cave, and karateka have the dojo. It's a fantastic physical and mental release from the pressures of life for a few hours—if you check your baggage at the door.

Practicing karate allows us to reap many benefits, including the increased ability to focus. However, some students walk in the door with issues that weigh on their minds during the entire class, sometimes to the point that the student is unable focus on the lesson and the details of training.

All of us are susceptible to the problem of bringing our baggage into the dojo—teachers and students, adults and children, male and female—no one is immune. If we're all vulnerable to mental baggage, how do we address the issues?

You see, another wonderful training benefit that is developed through our practice of karate is self-control. We have the ability, the will, and the choice to make a conscious decision of what we will allow into our mind at any time. This requires us to focus and practice controlling not only our actions, but our thoughts and emotions as well.

Every single time we step into the dojo, we need to make the conscious decision to leave our baggage at the door for a few hours, and focus our efforts on personal growth and progress.

Part 2. Habits — Here we will address the baggage of habits inside the dojo: training baggage. This often manifests in the form of previous training experiences and methods that the practitioner has learned while training in a different dojo or a different style.

This type of baggage is like a cold that just won't go away; it's a source of constant annoyance for both the student and the teacher alike. For the student to learn, the mind must be open and accepting of new or different methods. The cross-training or transfer student will at times "what if" the instructions because "we learned it like this at my previous dojo." While this isn't uncommon in new students, this juvenile behavior certainly is not conducive to progress; in fact, this type of thinking slows progress and growth. The practice of shoshin (beginners mind) is absolutely imperative when retraining or cross-training with methods that are different from those to which we are accustomed.

I personally like to use metaphors as a teaching aid, and I use this one for this topic: "It's like driving with the emergency brake engaged; you're moving, but you're slowing down your progress." So, drop the baggage by opening your mind and enjoy the ride.

It is vitally important for every student's progress to arrive at the dojo with an open mind, a closed mouth, and a sincere willingness to learn. Retain the knowledge from your previous style or teacher, but leave it at the door and empty your mind for new knowledge that your teacher is ready to share with you.

Fifteen

March 2014 was a special milestone for me. For months leading up to our dojo's fifteenth anniversary, thoughts have swirled and memories have surfaced. I've reflected and even questioned the effectiveness of time spent over the past decade and a half.

Have I done too little and not enough? Have I been overbearing or at times too soft? Have my admittedly harsh principles and standards driven students away, or attracted others to stay and train harder? Have my teaching methods been sufficient to transmit both physical and mental understanding of the details of our art to my students? How have I come this far, and how much further will I be able to go?

In a time when most would be enjoying this milestone in their martial arts life, I find myself questioning many things. My first thought is: am I sufficiently passing on my teachers' art to my own students? Takamiyagi

Sensei entrusted to me the propagation of Goshukan-ryu karate in the United States when he urged me to begin teaching in 1998. I didn't feel qualified then (I argued that point with him profusely before finally conceding) and I'm only slightly more comfortable now with the fact that my teacher had enough confidence in me and saw a future that, to me, was unimaginable at the time. Fifteen years later, I feel that I haven't done enough. I'm both humbled and driven by the heavy weight of responsibility that was bestowed to me as the first American representative of my teacher and his style.

> Another wonderful training benefit that is developed through our practice of karate is self-control.

As I write this, I'm struggling with putting the words down. I intended for this section to be a nice reminiscence of my first 15 years as the owner and instructor of the Columbus Dojo. But as I began writing, my thoughts began to change in midsentence. Perhaps I'll write another article on the subject, but for now I'm going to continue to write about what I'm feeling at this moment, so please be warned: if you enjoy my articles for the encouraging undertones, you may be disappointed with this one.

Lately, I've noticed the trend of karate students and teachers "shopping around" or jumping from dojo to dojo and even across different systems, styles, and organizations, all for the pursuit of paper promotions, titles, and recognition. Although this is becoming increasingly common, I have no tolerance for this type of behavior. What I have become as a karateka and a sensei can be attributed to two primary elements.

One: My teacher's guidance, leadership, direction, sharing, and tough love (boot in the rear) when I needed it. Takamiyagi Sensei is responsible for my first day as a teacher. Without him it would've never happened.

Two: My loyalty to my teacher and dedication to practicing and preserving the ways that he taught me. This loyalty has kept me on the path. No matter where I go from here, it all started with my teacher, who cares for me and trusts me enough to represent him and his art.

Over the past 15 years, there have been extremely challenging economic hardships that would have forced most dojo owners to close their doors; I'm both stubborn and loyal, so I (and my family) endured those tough times and the dojo stayed open. I owe a debt to my Sensei that can never be repaid (giri) but I am duty and honor-bound to continue teaching and sharing for as long as I am able. This hasn't always been easy or practical. The physical location of my dojo has changed many times over the past fifteen years, and during the most challenging time we went from a private dojo to a recreation center, City Park, and my backyard, all within one year. Times were hard then, and only the most dedicated students stayed; these students understand giri, and are the ones that will eventually be entrusted with the responsibility of passing our art to the next generation.

Over the past fifteen years, I have not accumulated a large number of students, nor one single plastic trophy. I have, however, been blessed with a handful of extremely loyal and fiercely dedicated students; they are my trophies. Their loyalty and dedication to the art, the dojo, and to me shine brighter than any plastic and chrome, and I am so very proud of them. I have also been blessed with a handful of very close friends, fellow teachers, and mentors that share my passion for the old ways—these people are my support system and shining examples for everyone to see and appreciate.

Over the past fifteen years, I've been blessed with a supportive wife and children that have been involved with so much more behind the scenes than most people ever see, and rarely appreciate. Although my children don't share the same level of passion for the arts that I do, they never complain, and they make me proud every single time they put their gi on and tie that obi around their waist. There have been times that I have been so discouraged and would have quit teaching if not for my wife's encouragement and intervention. For such a small, quiet woman, she has been a tower of strength and support to me in ways that are unfathomable.

Thank you, Takamiyagi Sensei, for teaching me, guiding me, and having faith in me to see what I couldn't see in myself. Thank you, Izumi, for being my rock and my unseen warrior in the shadows; thank you for always staying right beside me and only falling behind just to push me enough to make it over the hills and roadblocks. Thank you Erika, Lisa, Kaori, and Kenji for being wonderful children and fantastic students. You are an encouragement to me every day, and I love you all. Finally, thank you to each and every student that has ever allowed me to teach you; it is a duty and responsibility that I do not take lightly, and I'm looking forward with anticipation to your continued growth and development both in the dojo and in life.

Letting Go

Although this was written on New Year's Day, the message and principles are relevant year round.

Letting go. This has so many different meanings to different people—some positive, some negative, but always involving change.

In life, we often find it very difficult to make even the smallest changes, especially if this change involves disruption of our daily habits and lives. While I am a staunch advocate of holding on to the methods of times past, I have also been guilty of holding on for the sake of holding on. Maybe it's the fear of the unknown result that causes us to hang on for dear life to things, methods, and even people who have outgrown usefulness or even become toxic to our lives and livelihood. Very often, the negativity in our lives weighs us down, and before we realize it, we're being dragged down. This burden of negativity isn't always physical; we can also be dragged down emotionally, mentally, financially, and spiritually.

You may be wondering: Why now? Can't I wait until a more convenient time? *No.* There is no time like the present to take action! As people motivate themselves to improve their lives in many areas, one thing that is often overlooked is the simple act of letting go.

Understand that this is directed at me, the writer, even more so than it is to you, the reader. To you, this topic can be a simple reminder or a call to action. Whatever you get out of it is exactly what it is, and nothing more. To me, this is a reminder of a promise that I made to myself and to my family to cut negative processes and people from my life.

I'm letting go of the opinions others have of me—it doesn't matter, and I can't change it. I'm letting go of excuses—they're worthless and are one hundred percent counterproductive. I'm letting go of people—some are acquaintances with nothing positive to say.

I have quite a few goals this year for the improvement of my family, my dojo, and myself; I've decided that I will bring anyone with me that wants to improve themselves, but I won't be dragged down by any of them.

Be the Best

Martial art training is a journey, and for a select few it can be a very long and productive one. And like any long journey, we can expect twists and turns, hills and valleys, sunshine and storms, breathtaking views and sometimes views we would like to un-see. Of course, there will be potholes, bumpy roads, and the occasional roadblock too. All of these experiences are lessons that will collectively define our journey.

Although these roadblocks are memorable, they don't define our journey, they simply add contrast to the rich experience of our martial arts life. Think about it: if every day was sunny, beautiful, and worry-free, would sunny days be special? No. Without the occasional roadblock, and pothole (injuries, life events, and personal setbacks) our journey on the path of martial arts would be uneventful. Financial setbacks, health issues, injuries, and family and domestic problems are all very real challenges for all of us. Overcoming these roadblocks helps forge a stronger resolve. These challenges test the strength of our character, and when we have overcome these roadblocks; our sunny days are so much more enjoyable.

> It is vitally important for every student's progress to arrive at the dojo with an open mind, a closed mouth, and a sincere willingness to learn.

In the past, I have had several students that have faced real-life challenges to their physical health, and some experienced challenges to their finances. Some have faced other personal issues as well. Often, we are self-conscious when returning to training after a long absence. This feeling will sometimes cause students to shy away from returning to the dojo. To those I say, "Don't worry about catching up; be the very best *you* that you can be! Martial art training is very personal, and although we benefit greatly from the camaraderie and friendship of our dojo mates and martial arts family, we must each work to the best of our own personal ability to overcome our obstacles. Although we train side by side, no one can do it for us. Of course we encourage one another to keep pushing, and challenge one another to continue training, but at the end of the day *you* must be the very best *you*."

Some training is better than no training; come to the dojo and do what you can. The roadblocks will always come—don't be discouraged, and above all, don't let a little roadblock end your journey. There is no better feeling than climbing that hill and overcoming that challenge that has plagued you. Few things in life will make you stronger than rising to the challenge of adversity, and coming out on top with a glorious personal victory!

Challenges will come, health will fail; the sunny days are always so much better after the rain. Do what you can, no matter how little, and never, ever give up.

After the Rain

One morning, in the predawn hours, I was awakened by house-shaking thunder; not just a thunderclap, this was a barrage of booming thunder that shook the windows of the house, and set off car alarms. It was approximately 4:00am as I walked through the house and noticed something amazing—my children were all sound asleep! The cat had crawled into my daughter's bed, and the dog was whining outside; both animals were afraid of nature's fury, yet the kids weren't phased.

My wife and I both stayed up for a little while and watched the thunderstorm from the dining room window as the thunder rolled and boomed, and the wind howled through the trees. I must admit that I was very concerned as I watched the oak trees swaying violently as smaller branches began to snap off, just as the street started to flash flood before my eyes. I thought of the awesome, destructive power of the thunderstorm as I drifted back to sleep.

> ...we benefit greatly from the camaraderie and friendship of our dojo mates and martial arts family, we must each work to the best of our own personal ability...

A few hours later, we woke up to the most beautiful sunrise and a hauntingly quiet, calm morning. The sun began to peek through the clouds as the birds started their morning ritual of singing and chirping their good mornings to one another. A slight breeze was blowing through the leaves as the squirrels began to scurry for their breakfast, and the robins were scratching and pecking at the wet, soft earth for their morning meal. A brand new day had dawned. Balance had been restored, and life went on.

Friends, we can learn a lesson from children and nature.

The storms that we endure are not always shared with others around us, or even those very close to us. They remain content and unaffected and are oblivious to the storms that rage in our lives. This is good; those closest to us should not be subjected to the storms in our lives if they are not affected by them. Of course, there are times when this is unavoidable; our family and friends sometimes experience the storms with us. When this happens, we support and comfort each other through our storms.

Learn to move on; the past is the past. Throughout the storms, the squirrels and birds stayed safe and sheltered in their burrows and nests. After the storm, life went on. Animals don't complain to the other animals. Life goes on. Get breakfast, take care of the children, and repair the home. Move on.

When we endure the storms in our lives, these storms are frightening, stressful, and sometimes shake us to our core. But after the storm my friends, after the rain comes the beautiful sunshine peeking through the clouds. After the rain comes the new growth that could only be brought by the rain.

Our rainy days, our storms of life. . . they always come. The storms are unavoidable, but surviving them brings an experience that can't be shared with those who've only known sunny days. The strength and resilience that we gain by enduring the storms always seem to make the calm mornings so much sweeter. Life goes on after the rain.

Matsu

Strong, flexible, resilient.

These are the words that describe the *matsu* (pine) in Japanese. The pine is revered in Asian culture as a symbol of strength, longevity, and steadfastness.

Although the oak is mighty, strong, and hard, it cannot withstand heavy storms and wind—it will snap under its own weight. The pine tree, however, is flexible; the pine tree has an uncanny ability to bounce back from the worst storms. With branches broken and uprooted, the pine tree will send forth new growth. The roots will cling to rocks and cliffs. The pine tree doesn't just live, it thrives, bearing the scars of the gnarly trunk and twisted branches. The scars remind everyone who see it that this pine tree is a warrior—it weathered the storms, it was broken, and survived.

Friends, when the storms of life bring us down, let us remember to be like the pine tree, flexible and able to endure the storms. Although the storms of life may break us down, we each have the ability to bounce back, stronger than before. . . proudly bearing the scars that remind us how we have hurt, but are now healed.

Life is the journey between birth and death. Some endure it as a chore, while others really know how to live! What is our purpose in life? What does it mean to you? These are questions that we all ask and only you can answer it for yourself. While many people seek spiritual, psychic, or professional advice, the true meaning of life can only be realized by you when you have found and accepted your place in it.

My personal views on the meaning of life are shared on the following pages.

> Although the storms of life may break us down, we each have the ability to bounce back, stronger than before...

CHAPTER 11

Life

A Beautiful Thing

For something to lie dormant, useless and, for all practical purposes, dead to the world for months of bitter cold, what a spectacular vision it is to witness the rebirth of a single leaf! The process is quite breathtaking as we watch life sprout before our eyes from a seemingly dead twig or branch. As the temperature rises in the spring, reviving the slumbering sap, the very life-blood of the tree, it begins to circulate throughout the trunk, branches, and twigs. Before our eyes, new life is born.

Throughout the growing season, this will be a useful life; the single leaf in the photo accompanying this section is one of thousands on a fig tree in my back yard. In the coming weeks and months, the fig leaves will create a canopy of shelter for nesting birds, cool shade for my family and pets, and finally, in celebration of another successful growing season, it will produce sweet, luscious fruit that will feed birds and squirrels, in addition to providing the figs to make fresh, delicious jams and pastries for our family and friends. This process of renewal and growth happens everywhere, every spring, and we often overlook this spectacular transformation in pursuit of our busy daily lives. We overlook the growth process, but everyone wants to pick figs in the summer!

> Cherish your children, make time for them, and always, always keep your promises to them. These are lessons taught to me by my own father.

My son, in particular, loves figs. Like most nine-year-old boys, he can be impatient at times. While the leaves are still opening and growing on the fig tree, he is already asking when the figs will be ready. Yes, he already knows the answer—it's the same conversation we've had for the last couple years.

I say, "When the leaves are done growing, the fruit will begin to ripen. When the figs turn pinkish-purple, they'll be ready, and you can have all you want."

He smiles, and says, "I know, Dad, I was just asking."

In the pursuit of karate (and other forms of martial arts), careers, and relationships, people can sometimes be just as impatient as my young son waiting on his delicious figs—they want to enjoy the fruit before the growth! People want promotions and recognition in the dojo and in their careers; they want a perfect relationship with their dream man or woman. But people can often be impatient. Growth is often painful, stressful, and inconvenient, but growth is always rewarding. In the dojo, in our careers, in our relationships, and in life, we need to be patient and enjoy the growth process. In time, the efforts of our growth will be rewarded by the fruits of our labor. But until then, I encourage you all to enjoy the journey—because it's a beautiful thing.

Fishing

Everyone else was asleep as my son and I crept through the house in the predawn hours, preparing to go fishing at our favorite little fishing spot. My wife was up early brewing coffee for us (just because she's awesome) as we loaded up the rod and reels, tackle boxes, and buckets. I was still groggy—coffee in hand—while my son, Kenji, was grinning from ear to ear and bubbling with excitement.

As we were driving, we chatted about how many fish Kenji wanted to catch today. "Only five or 10, Daddy, that's enough for me," he said.

I smiled and nodded, "Ok son, you can do it. Catch your ten fish, and I'll help you clean 'em."

We arrived at our spot and cast the lines. Kenji, being only eight-years old at the time, still hadn't perfected the art of patience. He cast his line and promptly reeled it back in after 10 or 15 seconds. Kenji repeated this process a dozen times, and then complained that the fish weren't biting. I reminded him (again) to be patient.

After an hour or so with no bites, Kenji was ready to go home. We loaded the gear up and headed back home. I asked him if he was disappointed that we didn't catch any fish this morning.

"Not really, Daddy. I really just like fishing with you. I do like catching fish too, but I really just like going together."

I asked him why. "Well, it's just us boys, Daddy, and you take me to McDonald's, and I get to eat breakfast in the car while it's still dark, and that's kinda cool. And I like spending time together, Daddy, that's what I like the most." After that, I was the one grinning ear to ear!

As we unpacked our fishing gear, I began to think of the similarities between my son's approach to fishing and the traditional approach to *budo* (martial arts) training. We train with a very specific goal in mind, and while we should always strive for our goals, we also know that if we don't succeed the first time, we should always remember to be patient, and above all, enjoy the journey.

Last Sunrise

First, I want you to know that this is not martial-arts related. This is for my children. I hope you aren't disappointed, and I certainly hope that you aren't one of those that eat, sleep, and breathe martial arts while neglecting life's little treasures.

This morning, long before dawn, I was up making coffee. Although I was up all night, and in dire need of sleep, I scurried around the house preparing to take my children fishing as I had promised. My son was awake and waiting

on me when I returned home from work at 4:45am He smiled and said, "Daddy, I'm ready to go fishing!"

I said, "Me too, son!" He gave me a sleepy grin with a big hug and went to wake his sisters while I showered. After the coffee was made, we loaded the fishing rods, tackle, and buckets, then we were on our way.

We arrived at the pond and unloaded the gear in the predawn darkness. As the sun began to rise, I snapped the photo that you see here. I watched my children as they cast their lines over and over again, giggling and having a great time. I was so happy that I kept my promise to them. . . I thought of how blessed I am to have such wonderful children, and I reminisced briefly about the days before life became so busy.

Cherish your children, *make time* for them, and always, *always* keep your promises to them. These are lessons taught to me by my own father. During my entire childhood, he worked two, and sometimes three jobs to make ends meet. We didn't have a lot materially, but we wanted for nothing, and no matter how tired he was, my father always made time for us. I remember distinctly our day trips to Panama City Beach, Florida in the summers. I remember getting up before dawn and seeing my mother making sandwiches and Kool-aid to take to the beach for lunch. We arrived by nine or 10 in the morning and stayed at the beach all day, leaving in the late afternoon. I thought it was the greatest thing! What I didn't realize, until years later, was that we were poor, and although my father worked very hard, we simply couldn't afford to stay in a hotel for a few days. So we took a couple of day-trips to the beach in the summer. Why? Because my dad always kept his promises.

Our children won't care that we had to work late again, or that we were "just too busy." They will always remember the time that we spend with them and the promises kept or broken. As I write this, my mind is a little foggy and my eyes are burning; I have now been awake for nearly thirty hours, and I missed a little sleep but made another beautiful memory with my children. I hope they cherish our time together as much as I do. . . because someday we will see our last sunrise, and there are no do-overs.

Passing the Torch

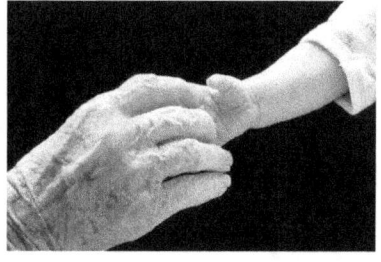

Since the dawn of time, the circle of life has continued. With each generation, the old pass their wisdom and knowledge to the young, before the light of the old is extinguished. Then the circle of life is renewed with each generation, until the young become experienced and wise, and as the next generation is groomed, the torch is passed once again.

In our community of Okinawan karate, 2012 was very difficult: we lost many great pioneers, experts, and ambassadors of Okinawan karate. These men have given their entire lives to spreading the wealth of knowledge that is gained through consistent practice of Okinawan karate, and in turn have touched thousands of lives in the process.

These great masters' lights shone brilliantly while they were with us; now their flames are extinguished, just as yours and mine will one day flicker into darkness. However, these teachers leave behind great students, masters in their own right, to carry the torch. The next part is very important, so pay attention.

Students—be loyal and dedicated to your teacher and your chosen *ryu-ha* (style). Earn the trust of your teacher by being sincere and faithful, and absorb all that you possibly can.

> These great masters' lights shone brilliantly while they were with us... these teachers leave behind great students, masters in their own right, to carry the torch.

Teachers—be loyal and dedicated to your students. Those that are loyal, dedicated, and sincere are very rare. Nurture them, teach them all that you know, and encourage them to learn more. These are the faithful ones that will carry on the torch for the next generation. Make sure it burns brilliantly!

BOOK THREE
LEGACY

Goshukan-Ryu Mon, created from the Takamiyagi family crest.

CHAPTER 12

Legacy

On this earth, we have a limited amount of time to make an impact—the average lifespan is between 60 and 80 years. During this time we live, love, work, create, and hopefully do something that will help and inspire the next generation. No matter our occupation, status, or income, every person leaves a legacy behind. Some folks work their entire lives in pursuit of building an empire, following a dream, or finding a cure. Others live simple, quiet lives and have their legacy thrust upon them in an instant, unplanned, unrehearsed, and unexpected. There are those rare occasions caused by a unique circumstance, luck, or tragedy over which we have no control. Yet most of the time we do have complete control over the direction of our lives. We sculpt and mold our future with our daily actions.

Takamiyagi Hiroshi, 29 years of age: 1969

Did the forefathers of Okinawan karate train and research with the intention of becoming immortal legends in the history books of karate? I don't believe they did, because that isn't the typical Okinawan way. Most of us will live our lives, raise our families, train and/or teach until we die, and that'll be it. No fanfare, no place in the history books, no style named in our honor, and no fancy titles. And that's perfectly ok. In fact, it's more than ok, that is a fantastic and fulfilling life.

If we train or teach with the sole purpose of chasing fame or becoming legendary, we have truly not learned the very basic lesson of humility. Some have already secured their place in history, others will be relatively unknown in life and death; but understand that fame has nothing to do with your legacy.

Legacy is what people remember about you. Legacy is the impact that is imprinted in the minds of all who come after you. Legacy is the result of your passion, your contribution, and ultimately your mark on society and your place in history. Three names that quickly pop into my head are: Gandhi, Mother Theresa, and Martin Luther King, Jr. These people created their legacy as a result of their unrelenting passion for a cause. It was never about money, power, or fame to any of them. They simply dedicated their lives to their convictions; the results were legendary.

This part of the book is dedicated to such a man: my teacher, mentor, and friend, Takamiyagi Hiroshi Sensei. His dedication and passion for karate, coupled with an unrelenting thirst for knowledge and his tireless search for the roots of Okinawan karate, led him down the path of personal growth and discovery that created his contribution and gave birth to his legend.

Takamiyagi Hiroshi and his mother Takamiyagi Kiyoko, 100 day photo: May, 1940

In the following pages, I will share with you, from my viewpoint, selected highlights of this man's life that have contributed to his place in history.

On January 30, 1940, Takamiyagi Hiroshi was born to Kiyoko and Jitsuji Takamiyagi on the island of Okinawa, the third son of five children. Little did he know that only a few decades later he would take the first steps to create his legacy. He studied Shuri-Te and Kobayashi-ryu as a student of Nakamura Ankichi.

Takamiyagi Naoki: Shuri-Te Bunkai Demonstration: 1983

Takamiyagi Hiroshi demonstrates Shuri-Te tuidi: kinawa 1980

Takamiyagi Hiroshi teaching bunkai: Hamagawa Dojo, 1981

He trained, researched, and represented his style and teacher through various methods, including public demonstrations and teaching in his own Shuri-Te Shibu Dojo in Chatan-Cho, Okinawa.

Research

In the 1980s, Takamiyagi Sensei met Lee Chee Ngai in Okinawa, as members of Friendship Society at *RyuDai* (Ryukyu University). Lee was a practitioner of *Wu Zhu Quan* (Five Ancestor Fist) and Takamiyagi Sensei quickly took an interest. After training in Okinawa with Lee, Takamiyagi Sensei traveled to Singapore to meet and train with Koh Nai Kheng, Lee's teacher. After months of intensive training in Singapore, he returned to Okinawa to continue training and honing his skills.

In 1988, Takamiyagi Sensei added Wu Zhu Quan to his curriculum, and changed

Takamiyagi Hiroshi demonstration of Passai kata: 1986

his dojo name to the Okinawa Goshukan Hamagawa Dojo, where he began teaching Wu Zhu Quan in addition to Shuri-Te Karate. This was the birth of Goshukan-Ryu and the confirmation of Takamiyagi Hiroshi as the pioneer and first Okinawan Karate teacher that brought Wu Zhu Quan to Okinawa.

As Takamiyagi Sensei continued his quest for more details of Wu Zhu Quan, his research led to the introduction of Alexander Lim Co, of the famous Beng Kiam Athletic Association in the Philippines. Much like himself, Co is both a warrior and a scholar, having

Koh Nai Kheng Sifu: Wu Zhu Quan (Five Ancestor Fist)-Singapore

Takamiyagi Hiroshi demonstrates Wu Zhu Quan: Hamagawa Dojo, 1988

Alexander Co and Takamiyagi Hiroshi, Manila, Philippines 1993

written and translated books on Five Ancestor Fist, Praying Mantis Kung-fu, and Filipino martial arts of Arnis and Eskrima in three languages. When Takamiyagi Sensei visited Co Sifu in 1993, he willingly and openly shared and taught Takamiyagi Sensei the details of his lineage of Five Ancestor Fist (Ngo Cho Kun).

Throughout the 1990s, Takamiyagi Sensei continued to train, research, and write articles on Wu Zhu Quan and the newly formed Goshukan-Ryu. Unlike other historical teachers that traveled to China and returned to Okinawa and blended Okinawan *Ti* with Chinese kenpo/chuan-fa, Takamiyagi Sensei kept the arts separate and taught them side by side, with the exclusive principles and concepts that were unique to both Shuri-Te and Wu Zhu Quan. From 2006 to 2008, after more than 20 years of dedicated practice and research of Wu Zhu Quan, he began creating a series of unique Goshukan-Ryu kata that highlighted the essence of both arts. These kata include: 1) Shokyu, 2) Renshuu, 3) Go-Shu Ken/Itsutsu Kubiken, and 4) Tairen Suiken.

In 2013, Takamiyagi Sensei made history once again by publishing the first-ever comprehensive book on Wu Zhu Quan in the Japanese language: *Go So Kenpo (Bibo Roku) Volume 1*. The book outlines the history and development of the southern Fujian Five Ancestor Fist style, his introduction to the system, and consequent research trips to Singapore and the Philippines. Additionally, both empty-hand and two-man forms are shared in detail, complete with step-by-step photographs. Elements of Shuri-Te and the Shuri-Te version of Chinto kata are also included in the text for comparison.

Making History Abroad

In October 2014, my teacher visited the US for the first time. In years past, we had discussed the possibility of Takamiyagi Sensei coming to America to teach, and on the eve of my dojo's 15th anniversary in early 2014, we both committed to make it happen. As a result of fundraising efforts by my dojo members and karate brothers, as well as a couple of very generous donations by some dedicated karateka and close friends, we were able to host Takamiyagi Sensei for three weeks of training at the Columbus Dojo with my students, and at the 15 anniversary Goshukan Gasshuku with karateka of different disciplines.

L-R: Ang Hua Kun, Christopher Ricketts, Takamiyagi Hiroshi, Alexander Co: Beng Kiam Athletic Association, 1993

Takamiyagi Hiroshi (Center) and Christopher Ricketts, Makati YMCA Philippines 1993

Junbi (Preparation)

The dojo was a whirlwind of excitement and hard training. I would be lying if I said that I wasn't nervous about my Sensei coming to see me at my dojo. Yes, I was very happy and extremely excited at the opportunity to host my teacher at my dojo and in my home, and quite thrilled at the promise of "catching up on corrections," as Sensei put it. I was ready to be evaluated, corrected, and even chastised for straying from the proper methods and execution of technique. In fact, after having not visiting Sensei for several years, I quite expected a *lot* of corrections!

Oh, but this was different! My Sensei would be in my dojo evaluating my students. The more I thought about it, the more nervous I became. Only 15 years prior, Takamiyagi Sensei had entrusted me as his representative in the United States. I was fully responsible for the proper and correct dissemination of Goshukan-ryu in America, and now it was time to find out if I was living up to Sensei's expectations and high standards.

I began to implement a more stringent practice of kihon, sometimes practicing 500, 1000, or 1500 repetitions in class. I began to "nitpick" the smallest details with my students' waza, and kihon practice—especially the seniors (black belts and brown belts). The students received the corrections well; they embraced the physical challenge, and they all worked extremely hard in anticipation of Takamiyagi Sensei's visit. Some were nervous, some were a little scared, but all of the students were excited!

Several months prior to Sensei's visit, I sent a package to him in Okinawa with several photos of us practicing and a few candid and posed shots as well. We spoke on the phone almost weekly and exchanged several letters as well. In one phone call, Sensei asked if was still practicing judo, and if I was teaching. I told him I still practiced a little, and that I taught my students basic *ukemi* (falling), *kansetsu waza* (joint locking techniques), and *shime waza* (chocking techniques) so that they would survive a violent throw if it happened. He then asked if we had mats down all the time or if it was just for the photos that I sent to him. Without going into the long history of the dojo and how far we had come in bringing that building up to code, but had run out of funds to repair the 120 year-old hardwood floor, I replied, "Hai Sensei."

He then casually mentioned, *"Ki ho ga ii dayo...ashi wa chanto tsukameru ne* (Wood floor is better . . . the foot can grip correctly)."

Again I replied, "Hai Sensei."

As I wanted my students to get the best instruction possible, we committed to repairing and refinishing the floor. All students pitched in, and a couple of the parents as well. We replaced old, rotten wood, we filled holes and cracks with wood putty, and we sanded a lot! We were only a couple of weeks away from Sensei's arrival when we realized that we wouldn't have enough funds to refinish the floor to its original condition. The repairs had been made, the floor was spot sanded, but we needed to rent a commercial drum sander to even out all of the waves, and high spots that happen over the course of more than one hundred years of use. The cost of the sander rental and the gallons of wood conditioner and stain were more than we could afford. All the funds raised were already allocated and there just wasn't enough to spare. At this point we were one week away from Sensei's arrival, and I called a dojo meeting. I thanked everyone for their hard training and their dedication after hours working on the floor repairs. One of my students suggested that we paint the floor as it was already sanded and would be fine to train on with a couple coats of primer and some heavy duty floor paint. We all agreed and Keith, one of my Yudansha, said that he could get primer and paint donated. So we moved forward with the plans. We picked up the donated primer and paint and stayed late a couple of nights to prime it. When the primer was dry, the sample of paint was laid down, but there was a problem. It was flat, and it wasn't floor paint.

We had come so far and were now only a few days away from Sensei's arrival. We needed approximately ten gallons of paint and we had to buy it. I explained to the students that we didn't have enough funds to finish the floor, and that we would just have to put the mats back down for now. We called it a night, and went home to rest. Later, my student Jeffrey contacted me and offered to go and pick up the paint to finish the dojo floor. I initially told him no, but he insisted and mentioned that he felt an obligation to help however he could to prepare our dojo for Sensei's arrival. At that moment, as a teacher, my heart swelled with pride; Jeffrey understood the concept of giri and was putting it to action.

USA Arrival

My wife Izumi and my son Kenji loaded up the truck for our late-night trip to the Atlanta airport to pick up Takamiyagi Sensei upon arrival. We talked and were buzzing with excitement during the entire ninety-minute trip. As we parked and made our way to the terminal, Kenji was skipping and hopping with energy to spare!

As I approached the stairs where he would be arriving from downstairs, I began to pace with nervous excitement. I looked at the arrival boards above the staircase dozens of times to check if Sensei's plane had indeed arrived, and minutes seemed like hours. A couple times I walked over to the baggage claim to ensure that he hadn't snuck past in one of the waves of people that had already disembarked from their red-eye flights, and indeed he hadn't. After a half hour or so, I finally saw Takamiyagi Sensei's face appear at the top of the stairs. He looked a little tired, but still had that quietly powerful presence that I remembered. . . the presence of a silent warrior.

I began to walk rapidly toward Sensei with my Izumi and Kenji at my side, and called out "Shinshii!" As I bowed deeply, he grabbed my hand and pulled me in for a hug, and said "*Hisashiburi Paka . . . Genki.*" After a quick reunion and hugs all around, we all made our way toward the baggage claim, talking as we walked, laughing and enjoying our quick reunion. We gathered Sensei's luggage, loaded it into the truck, and headed home.

Takamiyagi Sensei, Garry Parker, Kenji Parker at the Atlanta Airport: Atlanta, Georgia, 10/2014

My house is approximately ninety miles from the airport, so we had a great chat all the home; we laughed, reminisced about old times, told stories, and shared news. We finally arrived home just before 2:00am but were wide awake. After showing Sensei his room, we sat at the dining room table and began to talk. We spoke about the upcoming training schedule, his dojo and students, my dojo and students, karate history, lineage, and our mutual disdain for martial arts "politics." We had a some food, a pot of tea, then another pot of tea; we began to talk about kihon and the differences between *dento* and *gendai* karate with an emphasis on effectiveness and *tuidi,* which naturally led to an end of discussion and the beginning of training (at 4:00 am) A few hours later I was feeling the burn in my eyes and exhaustion began to replace euphoria. I suggested to Sensei that we get some sleep and start over fresh in the afternoon. He agreed, and we both retired to our respective rooms just before sunrise.

I had barely closed my eyes when I heard my wife's voice. "Sensei wants to know if you are awake yet." My eyes still burning, I got out of bed and looked at the clock on the wall. . . 9:00 am Less than three hours sleep and

Takamiyagi Sensei was wide awake, showered, and ready to train some more! I had two thoughts:

1. This is going to be a long and exhausting three weeks.
2. I hope I have that level of energy when I'm 74!

We had a cup of coffee, and then enjoyed a traditional breakfast of miso soup and rice, followed by quite a few cups of green tea. We chatted for a bit, and I gave Sensei a quick tour of the house, yards, and garden. As he looked around the neighborhood for the first time in the morning light, he commented how large everything was in America. One fact that even I had overlooked was that Okinawa has very few large, mature trees, due to the destruction of most of the vegetation during the Battle of Okinawa in WWII. In contrast, my neighborhood is full of large oak and pine trees that are well over a century old.

Back in the house, my living room was turned into a makeshift dojo for the next several weeks. Because my children were in school, it was both quiet and convenient. We quickly settled into a routine of breakfast, training until lunch, studying and discussion for an hour or so after lunch, and then training for a couple more hours. We did this on a daily basis during the week, and then trained at the dojo on Tuesday and Thursday evenings and early Saturday mornings. On Saturday afternoons, we would go sightseeing and restaurants.

Takamiyagi Hiroshi and Garry Parker at Parker's home; first morning in Columbus, Georgia: 10/2014

Sunday was usually more relaxed. We sat at the table for an hour or two after breakfast, sharing conversations about everything from training to family to the future of karate and Goshukan-ryu.

First Class

Our first class at my dojo with Takamiyagi Sensei was on Tuesday night, less than twenty-four hours after his arrival in America. We had planned a potluck dinner and demonstrations to commemorate the auspicious occasion. The students buzzed with excitement as they waited on our arrival. Sensei and I arrived early and there was already a large group of students gathered in front of the dojo anticipating meeting Takamiyagi Sensei for the first time. Everyone was all smiles, and a few seemed

Takamiyagi Sensei working on translations at the author's home: Columbus, Georgia: 10/2014

Takamiyagi Sensei making corrections for Parker's students at the Columbus Dojo: 10/2014

quite nervous, but soon got over it as we trekked up the stairs to the third floor to begin our training. Sensei had never watched me teach my own students, so he asked me to lead the training as we normally do so that he could observe. As we lined up and bowed in, the collective focus was more intense and the *kiai* (spirit shouts) were sharper that I had heard in recent months. After *junbi undo*, we began to practice kihon, and then a group kata

Takamiyagi Sensei teaches (author on the left) bunkai

Takamiyagi Sensei lecturing after the first class at the Columbus Dojo. Columbus, Georgia 10/2014

demonstration. We took a short water break after forty-five minutes or so and then resumed training. After the break, I asked Sensei if he would like to take the class, and he did for the next two hours!

Sensei made plenty of corrections, demonstrated *kata*, *tenshin* (body shifting), and principles of *tuidi* (grasping hands), and then we ended training to share a meal together. As most of the adults were sitting in my office, the training continued during dinner. At last, my students were able to realize, on a

Group photo after first class at the Okinawa Goshukan-Ryu Columbus Dojo: 10.14.2015

Takamiyagi Sensei teaching the author's son, Kenji. 10/2014

personal level, why I spoke so highly and respect so deeply my Sensei.

Appointment

At the end of the first class, Takamiyagi Sensei called me up to the front of the class for a presentation. Every promotion I earned had been in Okinawa, yet Sensei had decided to do this one in America, during his historical first

Takamiyagi Sensei presentation to Garry Parker: Appointment to Okinawa Goshukan-Ryu Karate USA Honbu Kaicho. 10/2014

visit, at my dojo and in front of my students. I stood in front of my Sensei in silence, attempting to process what was happening as he read the menjo and appointment.

On that day, Takamiyagi Sensei recognized my decades of loyalty to him, and to the art of Goshukan-ryu as he promoted and appointed me *Zen-Bei Okinawa Goshukan-ryu So Honbu Kaicho*.

The appointment was big, but the accompanying responsibility was a heavy

Takamiyagi Hiroshi and Garry Parker at Parker's Dojo. 10/2014

Takamiyagi Hiroshi and Izumi Shimabukuro-Parker. Audubon Park Columbus, Georgia. 10/2014.

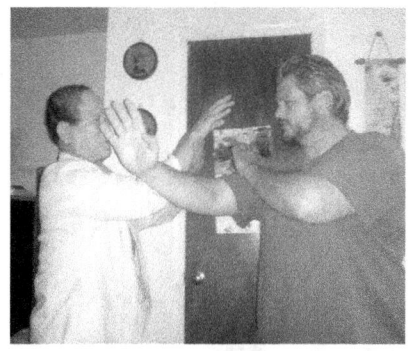
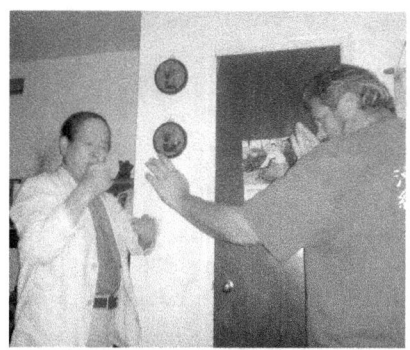
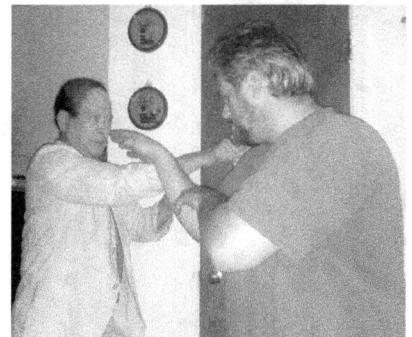
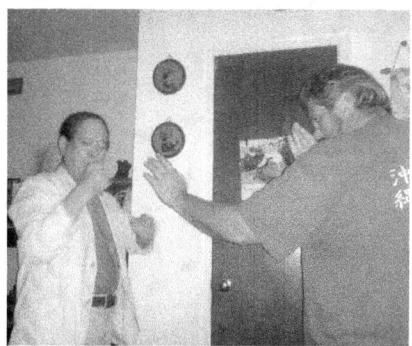

Takamiyagi Sensei and Garry Parker training Wu Zhu Quan Trapping methods at Parker's home in Columbus, Georgia. 10/2014

Takamiyagi Sensei and Garry Parker training kata and bunkai at Parker's home in Columbus, Georgia. 11/2014

load. The following weeks brought long conversations that outlined Sensei's expectations of me in the fulfillment of my duties and, quite honestly, I questioned if I was the right man for the job. Sensei reassured me that he had faith in me and was certain that I could overcome any obstacle that might arise. The result of this appointment brought an expansion and restructuring of our karate organization that has already began to flourish and grow. This is the legacy of a karate man: how far and wide he reaches to help others is

Parker and Takamiyagi Sensei at a sushi restaurant in Columbus, Georgia. 10/2014

Takamiyagi Sensei and the Parker Family at Sushi Restaurant in Columbus, Georgia. 11-2014

measured by those whose lives he has touched and molded.

In the weeks that followed, our home and dojo became a whirlwind of activity. Training, lots of training, early morning coffee and conversation, long productive mornings of private training, afternoons of sightseeing, museums, nature, and great food, and evening group training at the dojo where no one dared to miss a single class!

Takamiyagi Sensei enjoying Lasagna the night before returning to Okinawa. 11/2014

We trained in my living room, on the patio, in the backyard, outdoors in the park, on the banks of the Chattahoochee River, and in my dojo. Every training session was accompanied by extensive notes and copious amounts of green tea.

We enjoyed a good mixture of cuisine featuring Okinawan and Japanese food, as well as traditional American food. I have always known Takamiyagi Sensei to be a traditionalist, yet extremely open minded, and this was confirmed as he quickly found new "favorite" foods that he'd never tried before. Lasagna and salad for dinner, and biscuits with peppered gravy for breakfast became his most requested meals. Of course we still ate goya chanpuru (fresh from my wife's garden) Okinawa Soba, yakisoba, sushi, sashimi, gyoza, and plenty of rice, but life is about balance!

Gasshuku

The days flew by very quickly, and the fifteenth anniversary IOGKA Goshukan Gasshuku was upon us in the blink of an eye. I was humbled by the outpouring of love and support by the karate community and, in particular, my good friends, brothers and sisters in budo that came to learn and fellowship with us. Takamiyagi Sensei had a great time meeting and training with everyone and was genuinely interested in how everyone else trained, in that he asked several visiting instructors to join him in demonstrating their various bunkai of *Passai* kata as well as their *tokui* (favorite) Sai kata.

Throughout the long weekend, Takamiyagi Sensei exhibited the true Okinawan spirit of Ichariba Chodee, as he spent equal time teaching young children and senior instructors alike.

For many in attendance, this was their first opportunity to learn and train with an Okinawan Karate teacher; some weren't sure what to expect, and

Takamiyagi Sensei teaching on the Chattahoochee Riverbank at the Goshukan Gasshuku 10/2014

Takamiyagi Sensei teaching on the Chattahoochee Riverbank at the Goshukan Gasshuku 10/2014

Takamiyagi Sensei demonstrating Hama Higa no Sai.

Takamiyagi Sensei demonstrating Passai Sho tuidi.

Takamiyagi Sensei demonstrating Shuri-Te Tuidi.

Garry Parker demonstrating Wu Zhu Quan defense drills.

2014 Goshukan Gasshuku Group Photo: 10-18-2014

a few were quite nervous, but were soon put at ease as Takamiyagi Sensei began to teach and share with everyone. There were no invisible lines drawn, no limitations based on rank or experience. Everyone in attendance received equal opportunity to learn and train, and many of the visiting parents were surprised to find Takamiyagi Sensei spending extra time teaching and correcting the kyu-grades and younger children.

After three days of training, fellowship, great food, and exposure to Okinawan culture in the form of Taiko drumming and Eisa dancing, even the first-time attendees couldn't wait for the next Gasshuku!

2014 Goshukan Gasshuku- Mirai Kanai Taiko Performance: 10-18-2014

2014 Goshukan Gasshuku- Mirai Kanai Taiko Performance: 10-18-2014

2014 Goshukan Gasshuku- Mirai Kanai Taiko Performance: 10-18-2014

2014 Goshukan Gasshuku: Dojo owners/ Instructors Group photo: 10/17/2014

One Chance

Cha-do (Japanese art of tea) has a famous *kotowaza* (proverb) that has been adopted by many budoka: "*Ichi Go Ichi E* (one opportunity, one encounter; literal translation: this time only once)." The general idea is to seize every opportunity. Live in the now, appreciate what is within your grasp, and don't let it slip away, for you may never have this opportunity again. My relationship with Takamiyagi Sensei is condensed into this saying, in that I cherish every moment, every lesson, and every opportunity I have had to learn from him over the years. I take nothing for granted, and I cherish each training session as if it were my last. Although this is not an inherently Okinawan concept, it is steeped in the traditions of budo, and we can all certainly borrow this concept and learn from it.

One of my hobbies is creating original hand-carved Kanban (sign-boards); to commemorate my teacher's first historic visit to the United States, I created a Kanban with my favorite quote: Ichi go Ichi e, to present to Takamiyagi Sensei. I wasn't sure how he would feel about it since it wasn't specifically Okinawan, nor did the quote have karate roots; however, he was quite pleased when I presented it to him at the Gasshuku, and took a moment to give a speech about the meaning to him, and how it reminded him of our relationship and my dedication to him and the art.

One of my hobbies is creating original hand-carved *Kanban* (sign-boards). To commemorate my teacher's first historic visit to the United States, I created a

Kanban with my favorite quote, *Ichi go Ichi e,* to present to Takamiyagi Sensei. I wasn't sure how he would feel about it since it wasn't specifically Okinawan, nor did the quote have karate roots. However, he was quite pleased when I presented it to him at the Gasshuku, and took a moment to give a speech about the meaning to him, and how it reminded him of our relationship and my dedication to him and the art.

First Interview

The following interview took place in Columbus, Georgia in my home as we sat at the dining room table sipping green tea on November 2, 2014.

GP: Sensei, this trip to America is your first; have you thought about the historical significance of the creator of Goshukan-ryu teaching in the USA for the first time?

HT: Not so much (grinning), but I have been looking forward to this trip, and I'm happy to be here! I am pleased to see that your students are training very hard and are eager to learn more. It is obvious that the students at your dojo, and all of the karateka that attended the seminar (Goshukan Gasshuku), are serious karate students, and I enjoyed teaching and watching the different methods of the visiting instructor demonstrations.

GP: Thank you, Sensei. Your visit here is a dream come true for many, especially me. Can you tell me your impression of America?

HT: As expected, everything is so big here! I knew that the land area was larger and more plentiful, but the size of the trees here in Georgia really surprised me. The *Matsu* (southern pine) are so tall that I can't see the tops, and the oak trees are so thick and wide. Also, I was surprised to see so many squirrels running about; we don't have them in Okinawa. You know, in Okinawa we have very few large and old trees; most of them were destroyed in the war. So, yes, the large trees, wide-open spaces, and fields with wildflowers and vegetation that are near your house were quite a pleasant surprise. To see this on television or in pictures is not the same as experiencing it with your eyes; *subarashii dayo* (just wonderful)! I also enjoyed the museums and learning about your native culture in Georgia.

GP: Sensei, how were you introduced to Five Ancestor Kenpo (Wu Zhu Quan)?

HT: Well, I met a young man (Mr. Lee Chee Ngai) at *RyuDai* through the Okinawa-Chinese Friendship Society. As we began to talk, we discovered that we both were martial artists and decided to train together. What he showed me I had never seen before and it piqued my interest. Through researching the origins of the style, I realized that of all the southern Fujian (Minami Shorin) styles, Wu Zhu Quan is closer to the source of Okinawan Karate.

GP: Sensei, what drew you to research and eventually study Wu Zhu Quan?

HT: I became interested as I researched the possible roots of Okinawa Te and was initially drawn to the tsuru-ken (crane fist) aspects; I was also intrigued by the saru-ken (monkey fist) aspects, which I had not seen before. Later, as I began to learn and practice Wu Zhu Quan, I found the breathing and power-generation methods to be similar enough to be complimentary to Okinawan Karate.

GP: Sensei, can you please tell me about your study of Okinawan Karate?

HT: Yes. I began studying Goju-Ryu as young man, and later became a student of Nakamura Ankichi, one of Nakama Chozo's top students. After fifteen years of practice, I received a Shihan License in Shuri-Te, and opened a branch dojo in 1981. Initially, I was taught the methods of kobayashi-ryu, and after 4-dan, Nakamura Sensei began to teach me the older methods and tuidi of Shuri-Te.

GP: Sensei, what influenced your decision to combine the two styles of Shuri-Te and Go So Kenpo (Wu Zhu Quan) into a single ryu of Goshukan?

HT: For one, the two styles are not combined; they are both kept separate, but under the one banner of Goshukan-ryu. No kata, principles, or concepts have been added, subtracted, or blended. I have simply chosen to bring back to Okinawa the roots and possible origins of karate in an unaltered form. Also, the principles of relaxed power generation is very similar in both styles; as you know, breathing and power generation is the foundation.

GP: Thank you Sensei. By the way, you mentioned that nothing has been added or subtracted; have you done anything to help define Goshukan-ryu as a separate style?

HT: Well, I have created new and exclusive kata for Goshukan-ryu. These kata highlight both the Shuri-te and the Wu Zhu Quan methods and techniques. The first two kata are beginners-level kihon kata; they include such methods as *tegatana*, *shuto uke*, *tsumaki-geri*, and principles of *miji sagi* and *du ki naya*.

GP: How do you feel about kumite and full-contact training methods?

HT: To only practice kumite and forget about kata is unbalanced training; the smaller details of bunkai, especially regarding tuidi, cannot be grasped by those that only practice jiyuu kumite and ignore kata and bunkai practice. However, hard-contact kumite is a necessary part of the equation, along with kihon, kata, and bunkai training. Yes, there must be a balance. People that train in light contact or taiso (sport/point) only are ensuring failure as they are lured into a false belief that their waza and bunkai is effective without testing it. Especially problematic is a teacher with limited experience passing on false information to students.

GP: Sensei, what is necessary, in your opinion, for the future of Okinawan Karate to live on and thrive?

HT: Ah, this is the question! The current teachers must embrace the old ways of Dento Karate (pre-Itosu), or seek them out in order to be able to pass on the old ways to the next generation. Even in the age of gendai and taiso karate, the old methods must be embraced, even if they are no longer popular. It is our responsibility as teachers to preserve our Okinawan heritage for future generations to enjoy.

GP: Thank you Sensei; just a few more questions and we'll be done. Do you feel that Goso Kenpo (Wu Zhu Quan) and specifically Goshukan-ryu, will eventually be accepted on a large scale by the Okinawan Karate community within Okinawa?

HT: (Leaning in closely) If it is accepted or not is no great concern to me; this is not my goal, and this does not affect my research. People generally accept something when it becomes popular, with no regard to the validity or efficiency, or without concern of the historical significance. If Goso Kenpo and Goshukan-ryu are eventually "accepted," it should be on the merits of the art, not because of the art's growth and popularity.

As you already know, I distance myself from the politics of karate, and choose instead to focus on my research and training.

GP: Yes Sensei, I know that's true. One final question.

HT: Hai, dozo.

GP: Where do you see the future of Goshukan-ryu in five, 10, or 20 years?

HT: (He smiles, sits back in his chair, and points at me). That, Pa-ka, is up to you.

GP: *Hai, Wakarimashita. Ganbarimasu Shinshii.*

There were other questions asked during the interview that I am not permitted to disclose at this time, so they were omitted altogether. Hopefully this short interview will give you a little more insight into the ambitions of my teacher.

Going Home

The week prior to Takamiyagi Sensei's return to Okinawa was a whirlwind of activity with more training, assisting him with book content translation, and doing a photo shoot with Sensei for the second volume of Five Ancestor Kenpo. On the final day we trained a while, then sat and talked for hours until dinnertime. Sensei dressed for dinner and we all sat and had a long dinner, with more conversation and coffee. He issued words of encouragement and a call to action to my children to continue training hard and to behave themselves. Sensei commended my wife for doing so much to support me and expressed admiration for her being able to take care of me, the children, our home, and still have the energy to train. After dinner was over, we decided to get some rest for the long trip to the airport the next morning.

As Takamiyagi Sensei boarded the plane for his flight back to Okinawa, my wife and I stood in silence for a few minutes. It was a bittersweet departure, as we were extremely grateful for all that Shinshii had shared, both with me and with my students and guests. But I know he missed his wife and home, and I know that his other students in Okinawa missed him as well.

In the dim solitude of the airport parking garage at midday, I closed my eyes and heard the faint sound of the waves crashing against the jacks in Sunabe with the familiar twang of the *shamisen*, accompanied by the rhythmic beating of *taiko* (Okinawan drum) in the background. My nostrils flared slightly as I smelled that familiar aroma of salty air wafting on the breeze from the East China Sea, and for a moment. . . I was back home in Okinawa.

Epilogue

In the lifelong practice of karate, we will all leave a legacy behind. Some will know fame, some will become giants of their respective ryu. A few will become pioneers, and others will quietly influence the lives of everyone that is fortunate enough to know them through words, deeds, and action. No matter the quantity of students, accomplishments aren't necessarily measured in numbers; we'll be remembered for our passion, our convictions, and the people that we helped or influenced. Some will have a room full of trophies, titles, and medals; others will have thousands of students or a large bank account. Even fewer will have nothing tangible to show for all their hard work; there will be no accolades, no trophies or medals, and perhaps only a few students, but they have developed phenomenal skills through tireless practice and research. Great or small, everyone leaves a legacy. What will yours be?

My life thus far has been colorful, exciting, and full of surprises. There have been steep hills and deep valleys, raging storms, and spectacular sunsets along the way. Every experience adds another page, another chapter, and another story to my life's journey.

No matter the direction, and no matter what the future holds, I will always enjoy the *chanpuru*—the experiences, people, and events that have been seemingly thrown together in chaotic harmony that makes up the unique and exquisite flavor of my life.

Nuchi Du Takara . . . Life is a treasure.

Glossary

Awamori—Distinctively Okinawan rice liquor.

Bokken—Wooden practice sword

Bento—Premade boxed lunch usually with meat or fish, fresh vegetables, and rice.

Bonenkai—Japanese end-of-year party. Literally "forget the year."

Budo—Japanese martial arts. Literally "martial way."

Bugei – Traditional martial arts

Bushido Shoshinshu – Code of the Samurai

Bujutsu—Japanese martial arts. Literally "martial practice."

Chabidasai—Forgive the intrusion (Okinawan language).

Cha-do—Japanese art of making green tea.

Chanpuru—Something mixed together. Also the name of a popular dish in the Ryukyus.

Chuan-Fa—Chinese language: Fist Law; Kenpo in Japanese language.

Chi-ishi—Strength stone, Okinawan karate strength-training tool.

Chikara-ishi – Strength stone, Okinawan karate strength-training tool.

Daijiyoubu—It's ok.

Dai-sensei – Lit. Great Sensei: the leader of a particular ryu/style

Dan—Black belt rank.

Dento—Classical.

Deshi—Student.

Do—Way or path.

Dohai—Peer, someone of the same rank or status.

Dojo—Place of the way, for martial arts training.

Edamame—Soybeans in the pod (steamed and salted).

Eisa—Traditional Okinawan dance during Obon used to pay respects and "wake" ancestors.

Gaijin—Foreigner (non-Japanese).

Gajimaru—Banyan tree (Okinawan language).

Ganbatte—Do your best!

Gasshuku—Literally, "come together." Martial arts training event, usually held outdoors and lasting several days.

Gendai—New/modern martial arts systems.

Genki—Health or healthy.

Geri/Keri—Kick/to kick.

Giri—Obligation, duty.

Gijutsu – Skill or technique.

Gomen nasai—I'm sorry, an apology.

Goshin-jutsu—Self-defense arts.

Goshukan-Ryu—The martial arts style comprised of Goso Kenpo (Five Ancestor Fist) and Shuri-Te.

Goso Kenpo—Japanese phonetic reading of Five Ancestor Fist.

Gurugun—Native fish found in the waters of the Ryukyu Islands.

Haisai—Common greeting in Okinawa.

Hakama—Skirted, pleated, trousers. Formally worn with kimono or with uwagi for koryu budo practice.

Hamaya Soba—A local favorite Soba restaurant in Okinawa.

Hanshi – Highest level teaching license in Karate: typically awarded at 9th Dan.

Hisashiburi—It's been a while. (Long time, no see).

Iaido—The practice of drawing and cutting with the Japanese sword.

Iaihyodo –The practice of drawing, cutting, and *kumitachi* (partner training) with the Japanese swrord.

Iaijutsu –The martial aspect of Iaido emphasizing combat training.

Ichariba Chodee—Okinawan maxim: Once we meet, we are brothers and sisters.

Ichi go Ichi e—Cha-do influenced maxim: One chance, one opportunity. Seize the moment.

Ippon kumite—One-step fighting drills.

Ishi-bako—Literally, stone box – used for strengthening and conditioning fingers.

Izakaya—A restaurant and pub-type establishment popular in Japan and Okinawa.

jiyuu kumite – Free fighting.

Joto—Very good.

Junbi—Prepare.

Junbi Undoh—Prepatory exercise(s).

Judo—Gentle art/way.

Judo-ka—Judo practitioner.

Jujutsu—Soft/pliable art.

Jutsu—Tactical art, or literal method. The practice of something.

Kaisha—Company or workplace.

Kaizen—Consistent improvement.

Kanban—Sign or signboard. Traditionally wooden with carved or painted lettering.

Kanpai—Cheers!

Kansetsu—Joints (neck, wrists, elbows, shoulders, hips, knees, ankles).

Kantoku—Coach.

Karaoke—Literally "without vocals/voice."

Karate—Literally, "empty hand." The martial art created on the Ryukyu island of Okinawa.

Karate-ka—A karate practitioner.

Kata—A prearranged pattern of defensive and offensive techniques that are practiced to learn the core of a style.

Katana—Japanese sword.

Katsuo—Dried, shaved bonito fish. Used for seasoning in soups and broths and as a topping for tofu.

Kazoku—Family.

keikogi—This definition is below.

Kiai—Spirit yell.

Kihon—Basic techniques.

Kendo—Japanese martial sport where armor and bamboo swords (shinai) are used.

Kenjutsu—Japanese sword arts.

Keiko—Training.

Keikogi—Training uniform.

Kenpo—Literally "Fist Law."

Kodomo—Child/children.

Kohai—Junior (ranked).

Kotowaza—Popular Japanese saying or quote.

Kumite—Controlled fighting or sparring with rules.

Kyoshi—Master Level Licensed Instructor

ma-ai—the concept of gauging distance

Makiwara/Machiwara—Striking post, traditionally wrapped in rice straw. Modern versions are wrapped in leather or rope.

Manzamo—Cliff of one thousand seats.

Matsu—Pine.

Matsuri—Festival.

Mawashi—Circular or round.

Mensore—Welcome (Uchinaaguchi).

Mushin—Empty mind. Focused with no specific thought.

Mugai-ryu Iaido—A popular Iaido style

Nafudakake – Name boards.

Naicha—Mainland Japanese person (Uchinaaguchi).

Nakanomachi—Entertainment district in Koza, usually off-limits to foreigners.

Nifedebiru—Thank you (Okinawan language).

Nigiri-ga-me—Gripping jars.

Nihongo—The Japanese language.

Ngo Cho Kun—Cantonese pronunciation, Five Ancestor Fist.

Nuuchi Du Takara—Life is a treasure (Okinawan language).

Obasan—Old woman.

Obi—Belt.

Obon—Festival to honor the dead ancestors.

Ojisan—Old man.

Okinawa—The largest and main island in the Ryukyu Island Archipelago.

Pa-Ka—Japanese pronunciation of Parker.

renzoku kumite—Continuous fighting.

Ronin—Literally, "wave man." An unemployed Samurai.

Ryu—Style or system (martial arts).

RyuDai—Abbreviaion for Ryukyu Daigaku.

Ryu-ha—Style and school or sect.

Ryukyu—The name of the southernmost islands of Japan; formerly an autonomous kingdom with ancestry in China.

Sakurami—Cherry-blossom viewing.

Sashi—This is not a stand-alone term. It is used with the prefix 'Ishi' for Ishi-sashi (stone lock)

Seiza—Traditional Japanese style of sitting with legs folded under the body.

Senjutsu—Tactical strategy.

Senpai—Senior in rank, age.

Sensei—Teacher.

senjutsu – This definition is three lines above.

Seppuku—Ritual suicide.

Shamisen—Native three-stringed instrument of Okinawa, similar to a banjo.

Shibu—Branch.

Shibumi—Simple elegance.

Shihan – Licensed Master Instructor.

Shime—Closing or choking.

Shin—Heart or mind.

Shinshii—Okinawan language for teacher.

Shodan—Beginning level of black belt rank.

Shomen—

Shoshin—Beginner's mind.

Shujutsu—Front of the Dojo: Place of respect that usually houses the photos of past masters.

Sifu—Chinese language for teacher.

Soba—Noodle soup (in Okinawa, usually thick buckwheat noodles seasoned with bonito broth).

Soki-soba—Pork spare-rib-flavored noodle soup. Distinctly Okinawan.

Subarashii—Wonderful.

Sunabe—Literally, "sandy beach." Oceanfront area in the Miyagi area of Chatan in Okinawa.

Sunabukuro—Literally, "sandbag." Used for striking and kicking.

Suna-kake—Sand throwing. Techniques used to blind an opponent by throwing sand with the staff or oar.

Taikai—Competition or tournament.

Taiko—Okinawan drum.

Tanren—Severe training. Used in reference to pushing past your own preconceived limitations.

Tenshin—Body shifting, moving off-center to avoid and redirect an attacking opponent.

Ti—Okinawan language for hand; indigenous martial art.

Tsukemono—Pickled vegetables or light foods.

Tsunahiki—Tug-of-war with a giant rope; annual event in Okinawa.

Tuidi—Literally, "Grasping hands." Methods of karate that usually end in pain-compliance submissions.

Uchinaa—Okinawan language for the island of Okinawa.

Uchinaguchi—Okinawan language.

Uchinanchu—Native Okinawan person/people.

Ukemi—Falling and rolling (judo/jujutsu).

Uwagi—Training top/shirt.

Wakarimasu—I understand.

Waza—Technique.

Yudansha—Black-belt ranked martial arts practitioner.

Zanshin—Literally, "remaining mind." Vigilance, extreme awareness.

Zen—Literally, "all (encompassing)."

About the Author

Garry Parker was born in Columbus, Georgia, and began training in Kodokan Judo as a high school student in 1984. After high school graduation, he enlisted in the United States Air Force and was stationed at Kadena Air Base, Okinawa, Japan. Shortly after his arrival in Okinawa, Parker enrolled in the Hamagawa Dojo, where he learned under the watchful eye of Takamiyagi Hiroshi, Hanshi, the founder of Goshukan-Ryu Karate. After separation from the Air Force, he was granted a visa and continued to live and train in Okinawa until 1996, when he moved back to his native Georgia in the United States. Parker received authorization to teach Goshukan-Ryu in America and in 1999 opened the first branch Okinawa Goshukan-Ryu Dojo outside of Okinawa.

As the senior American student of Takamiyagi Hiroshi, Mr. Parker serves as the North American *Honbu-Cho* (director) for Goshukan-Ryu Karate. He also hosts the annual Goshukan Gasshuku, and teaches at regional training camps and seminars as he works passionately to spread his teacher's art and the values of Okinawan Karate and *Wu Zhu Quan* (Five Ancestor Kenpo).

He is the pioneer of Okinawa Goshukan-Ryu Karate in North America and is the author of dozens of articles and other books, including, *Hidden Treasures: Discovering the Secret Dojo*. He has worked in the private security industry, honing his skills in the tactical training field, in addition to being a small business owner and a corporate trainer.

TAMBULI MEDIA

Excellence in Mind-Body Health & Martial Arts Publishing

Welcome to Tambuli Media, publisher of quality books on mind-body martial arts and wellness presented in their cultural context.

Our Vision is to see quality books once again playing an integral role in the lives of people who pursue a journey of personal development, through the documentation and transmission of traditional knowledge of mind-body cultures.

Our Mission is to partner with the highest caliber subject-matter experts to bring you the highest quality books on important topics of health and martial arts that are in-depth, well-written, clearly illustrated and comprehensive.

Tambuli is the name of a native instrument in the Philippines fashioned from the horn of a carabao. The tambuli was blown and its sound signaled to villagers that a meeting with village elders was to be in session, or to announce the news of the day. It is hoped that Tambuli Media publications will "bring people together and disseminate the knowledge" to many.

www.TambuliMedia.com

www.ingramcontent.com/pod-product-compliance
Lightning Source LLC
Chambersburg PA
CBHW052031070526
44584CB00016B/1995